ADVANCE PRAISE FOR A

"Maren Higbee is a master storyteller and a pragmatic optimist, and her wildly entertaining new book is the perfect dose of humor and strength for caregivers looking for a path forward. *A Cancer Patient's Wife* is as much a way of life as it is a book; we are lucky to have Maren as our guide."

—Ashley Yesayan, CEO and founder of OneVillage.io, and cancer survivor and caregiver

"*A Cancer Patient's Wife* will walk you through all of the human emotions, with laughter and tears. From the moment of diagnosis to post treatment, it details the ups and downs of caring for someone you love who is going through trauma, NONE of which is easy. Cancer affects everyone in the household, and holding your partner's hand, even when they are angry and want to be alone, is incredibly hard. Maren portrays this journey with honesty and gives hope to others who may be walking the same path. A must read for loved ones of someone recently diagnosed."

—Michelle Beck, host of the *Breast Friends Cancer Support Network* podcast, author, patient advocate, and two-time breast cancer survivor

"A heartwarming and sometimes heartbreaking novel, *A Cancer Patient's Wife* offers a rare and intimate glimpse into a caregiver's life. In this provocative story of struggle, frustration, and love, the reader is thrown into Maggie's world as her husband, Luke, begins his journey with cancer."

—Martina Dalton, author of the Clarity Bloom series

"*A Cancer Patient's Wife* is the touching story of Luke and Maggie, a husband and wife who practice 'laughter is the best medicine' when Luke discovers a cancerous tumor, which they name Arnie. As the treatments continue and Luke becomes weaker, their sense of humor does too. But the crazy antics of Maggie's drunken sister bring laughter back into their lives and is a welcome break in the serious drama that continues to unfold. This novel is a wonderful story of the hardships a caretaker encounters when attending to a loved one with a life-threatening disease, but also is a roadmap to surviving it."

—Brenda Beem, author of the young adult fiction series *Knockdown, Beached,* and *Anchored*

A CANCER PATIENT'S WIFE

A

CANCER

PATIENT'S

WIFE

A NOVEL

MAREN S. HIGBEE

Patterbee Publications
Marenhigbee.com
Seattle, WA, USA

Published 2023

Library of Congress Control Number: 2022951980

ISBN: 978-1-63315-312-7 (paperback)
ISBN: 978-1-63315-330-1 (e-book)

Editing by Erin Parker
Proofreading by Lynn Slobogian
Cover and interior design by Jazmin Welch (fleck creative studio)
E-book production by Legible Publishing Services
Project management by Carra Simpson

For my love, Brandon.

To the Swedish Cancer Institute team and oncology workers around the globe. You each help make the unbearable bearable. Thank you.

Diagnosis

1

I NAMED MY HUSBAND'S TUMOR ARNIE. I assumed this mass was likely some random fat cell gone wild. My husband, Luke, was a healthy forty-four-year-old. Now the little bastard, Arnie, had made us spend Friday night in this dirty hospital emergency room. How would they get rid of Arnie, anyway? Surgery? I hoped it wouldn't be too dangerous.

You'd think it would be difficult to shock me, a former reality TV producer. But today had done it. The drug-addicted wannabe stars literally throwing ice at me had nothing on this tumor. Luke had gone to the doctor with a tickle of a cough and ended up in the emergency room, meeting that jerk, Arnie, who was busy pushing Luke's right lung and esophagus aside, like last night's tuna casserole.

Was that tuna casserole I could smell drifting through the room as I waited? No, it couldn't be. Everyone knows to not heat tuna, or any kind of fish, in a public microwave. Could someone be that rude in the emergency room of all places?

For that matter, who the hell eats tuna casserole anymore? Not me, that's for sure!

My internal musings about tuna were interrupted as Luke was rolled back into our room. Relief rushed over me when I saw those warm brown eyes and a calm smile. Our eyes met, and I grabbed his hand.

"Do you smell that nastiness?" I asked, avoiding the more pressing questions.

"Fish. Your favorite!" He grinned, then looked away. "So much for something simple like pneumonia." We laughed, unsure of how to behave.

Instead of discussing our concerns, we decided to make this fun. First, we took a picture of Luke's hairy chest, which was missing four square patches where the heart monitors were seated. Next, he faked surprise as he showed off one cheek through the crack in the back of the hospital gown. We agreed that the hospital gown was craving a makeover; the designer could have found a more lively pattern than faint blue squares.

Once we finished the photo session, we noticed a tall doctor standing in the doorway, watching. When we made eye contact, he approached, saying many words that became a jumble. The only ones I actually heard were "could be cancer."

We sat in stunned silence. How had we ended up here? We looked at one another, then back to the doctor as if we were in a slapstick comedy. *This can't be happening*, I thought. We were about to celebrate our fifth wedding anniversary. In our early forties, we were too young for cancer, right? This kind of thing happened in your eighties, not now. Not just as we were starting our life together.

"'Could be'?" I asked once my head cleared enough for words to be possible again. "What are the chances that this tumor is not cancer?"

The doctor stared at the gold-specked floor. His head shook from side to side. No, not in disapproval at the dirty floor. Staring at the floor meant no, Arnie was cancer.

"What is the prognosis?" I asked.

"We won't know until all the tests are complete. For now, we have to be patient." He looked away again.

"For how long? Will he need surgery?"

He shrugged. "We'll start tests on Monday, and it will take four to five days to get the results."

My stomach dropped. A week? Seriously? How could I wait a week? How could Luke wait to know if he had six days, months, years, or decades left? How? And what about me? What if he died?

I felt like I might throw up.

What happened next was a blur to both of us. More words floated around the room. People buzzed around Luke's bed. The only thing we both knew was that our lives had just changed forever—all due to some six-inch unidentified mass named Arnie.

2

IN THE 1990 MOVIE *KINDERGARTEN COP,* there's a funny scene in which Arnold Schwarzenegger, upon being bombarded by the curious questions of a classroom of children, rubs his head in exasperation. The kids chime in with diagnoses. "It's not a tumor!" he shouts, frustrated as if that should be obvious.

I named Luke's tumor Arnie because that's how I felt. I was certain that someone would make a mad dash into the room and say, "Whoops, wrong X-ray. That dark mass and fluid in your husband's lung is actually a bad case of pneumonia, not cancer. Sorry." That moment never came. You know your life has taken some crazy twist if you're hoping for pneumonia.

Before this, I had sometimes wondered about pivotal moments in some people's lives. Like when an amputee learns they've lost a limb. Or when a coma patient wakes up only to realize a year has passed.

Or when you learn someone you love has cancer.

Now I knew how that last one felt, and it was not good. My thoughts went in a million directions. I grabbed Luke's hand to stabilize myself. I looked into his eyes, wondering what was happening in that amazing brain. How was he feeling? I loved this man so much it hurt. There is nothing like a dose of Arnie to remind you how good your life is. Or was.

We'd flown kites on the beach in Lincoln City, Oregon, only two weeks ago. Our dog, Westy, chased the waves while we raced around, trying to keep the kites high in the air for as long as possible on the vast windy beach. At the time, I hardly noticed how much Luke was struggling. He is much more talented than me at kite flying, but his kites were crashing into the ground more than mine. He was out of breath. I am usually the weaker, physically challenged one. Now that I was thinking about it, he'd also had trouble climbing the small hill back to our Airbnb, and I didn't. Luke and Westy usually charged up hills like mountain goats with nonstop energy while I dragged behind, panting and taking breaks. This time he'd been the turtle to my sloth. Why had I just shrugged these clues off? Could I have saved or helped him if I'd paid more attention and taken action then? My eyes welled up with tears. I wiped them away, hoping he didn't see.

I kept looking at Luke, knowing this strong, calm, reserved man would process his some-kind-of-cancer diagnosis silently. Still I hoped that maybe, just maybe, he would be able to share his feelings with me. I wanted to ask Luke questions, but, miraculously, this chatterbox of a wife couldn't find any words. So we just sat, holding hands, and stared at the blank cream-colored emergency room walls listening to the beeping and bustling happening outside the doorway.

After about twenty minutes, our silence was interrupted by a nurse. She was a tall Black woman with a smile pushing an even bigger wheelchair.

"Wow, that's huge!" Luke said, staring at the double-wide wheel-chair. "Can I just walk?"

"Nope, sweetie, you can't. We need to keep you overnight for observation and get that heart rate down. It's racing, and that is dangerous. But here we can handle it, and you'll be safe. Now, sit down, please," she said in a kind yet assertive tone.

"He needs to stay overnight? One night or more?" I quickly looked at Luke to gauge his reaction.

"We have to observe him first. Then we'll know. But I promise this is the safest place for him." She smiled and squeezed my shoulder.

I continued to stare, picking at my fingernails. Luke seemed unfazed. He plopped his five-foot, six-inch frame into the oversized chair. It could have fit both of us and our ninety-pound German shepherd dog.

Once Luke was seated, off we went. She rushed us through a maze of hallways for about ten minutes. Finally, the elevator doors opened to a shiny ONCOLOGY sign announcing our destination in this massive hospital. I gulped and stood there for a moment. How the hell had this become my life?

The nurse wheeled Luke along and spoke enthusiastically about the team he would meet here in Oncology. I paused. My feet felt stuck. "Oncology," I said, looking at the brushed silver letters sharing a cold and terrifying message. *Oncology*. The vast wall behind the word was cream with a blue line twisting its way through the background, adding a touch of color to the foreboding term. That shape reminded me of the whisper of a word. I didn't know if I wanted to cry, scream, or just faint. *Oncology*. No, this couldn't be a word that pertained to us. Could it? Luke and I didn't have this word in our vocabulary right now because we were both healthy. Weren't we? This was a dream, an awful dream. *Oncology*. I touched the large *O* and felt its chilly circle. I imagined it squeezing the life out of my finger.

The spell was broken by a gentle hand on my shoulder. "Are you okay?" a nurse with kind blue eyes asked.

"Oh, yeah . . . I'm just here with my husband. Shit! Where is he?"

"I've got you. My name is Lara. I'm one of the nurses here and will help you with anything you need. Luke is just down the hall. I'll take you there." She kept her hand on my shoulder until we arrived. "You need anything else?"

"Is he going to die?" I asked, voice shaking.

"We need to gather more information before we make any conclusions. I know it's tough to do this but try to trust the process."

"So, he might?" Nausea gripped my stomach so tightly I nearly doubled over.

"Let's gather information and do our best to get him healthy. He's young, and that's great. Can I get you some water or juice?"

I shook my head and paused at the door. Since Lara wouldn't reassure me, now I knew losing my husband was a real possibility. I closed my eyes and imagined the ocean, trying to breathe with the waves coming in and out. Lara just stood next to me until I was ready. I pushed the door open and saw his cute face. I wondered if Luke knew that he might die.

Inside, Luke stood by the window staring at Seattle's skyline. It was dark now, so we could see all the lights glimmering in the distance.

These distant twinkles were an echo of a happier time. They reminded me of a recent dinner for his forty-fourth birthday. Luke's parents, now retired to Australia, had been in town for the final sale of their house. We treated them to Luke's favorite dinner of popcorn shrimp, king crab leg appetizer, steak, and mashed potatoes, finishing off with a coconut ice cream sundae adorned with two candles: one for Luke's birthday and the other to celebrate his parents' new adventure. Luke and his dad had a heated discussion about the best whiskey to use in an old-fashioned, so I had a rare opportunity to chat alone with his mom, Judy.

Since I had lost my mother years ago, I ached for that connection, the love that comes specifically from a mom. Judy and I only talked about small things, like the ingredients of each dish as we took our first taste and the design of the restaurant overlooking these stunning lights. But through that simple conversation and the way she looked at me, I had known she was there not only for Luke but for me as well. At the end of the night, as we waited for the valet to deliver our cars, she hugged me and whispered in my ear, "You know I love you like my very own daughter, yes?" I had held her, inhaling the smell of her gardenia lotion, soaking in that motherly love, and nodded. I missed Judy more than I thought possible.

Motherly love. I sighed. Oh no. His mom! Judy already had the weight of the world on her shoulders, caring for her husband of nearly fifty years, who'd fallen ill with pneumonia on the way home from visiting us and was still struggling to breathe to this day. How would we tell her that Luke was now very ill too? What if she blamed me? I didn't know if I could take any upset from anyone right now.

Stop, I thought. *I can't share the news until I actually have information to share.*

I snapped back to the tiny hospital room where the love of my life stood. He stared out the window as if pondering his life. Was he wondering if he would be here in five years, one year, one month, or even next week? All we knew was that it was a six-inch mass and cancer, but that could mean chemo, surgery, or something terminal. My heart ached. I blinked away my tears because this wasn't about me right now. This was about the man across the room—the one who was facing his mortality—who was slowly turning to look at me for support.

3

THE STRANGE SILENCE BETWEEN US was a sign that we were both contemplating the mystery of what would happen to our lives as we set off on this new cancer journey.

Luke finally broke the stillness. "At least we got a room with a view for our Friday night date."

"Yeah, but the spread here leaves a bit to be desired." I flapped the hospital menu toward him. "Can you believe that nurse told me that they cover your food but not mine? I'm the lady here. The nerve."

"I told them you were a picky eater, princess."

We laughed. Luke changed back into his street clothes. He then took the neatly folded hospital gown, socks, and robe from the stack on the bed and stuffed them into the farthest corner of the room. He was getting them out of his line of sight—a silent protest. Luke refused to appear sick, so he wouldn't dress like he was. Once the offending garments were gone, Luke lay on the bed in the jeans and button-up shirt he'd been wearing when life was still normal. It was hard to believe that was only five hours ago.

"Hey there, suave. What are you doing with that sexy gown? No more fashion shows for me? But you looked so cute with your butt peeking out."

"Oh, you liked that, did you?" He winked. "I'm not going to be comfortable in that so I won't wear it."

We settled in to watch TV.

After we'd waited a few more hours, a doctor appeared in the doorway to tell us they would do more tests the following day. A nurse checked Luke's vitals and offered to bring me a cot if I wanted to spend the night. Luke's expression gave no clues about his wishes. Did my introverted husband want to be alone or not? If it were me in the hospital bed, I'd want company. But this was Luke. It had become abundantly clear long ago that we processed information in entirely different ways. Any time I had a heated argument with my sister, Ronnie, afterward I'd tell Luke all about it, my words spilling out as if from a broken water pipe. In comparison, on the rare occasions that Luke let my sister get under his skin, he became quiet and distant, making his way to the basement to tinker with anything he had down there: lawn mowers, Weedwackers, or even a broken mechanical dog the neighbor kid brought over to be fixed. He'd keep to himself until he genuinely had a factual statement to share with me.

"So, honey, how are you? Really?" I asked on the off chance he'd tell me what he wanted.

"Don't be alarmed, love, but I might—just might—have cancer." He smirked.

"Oh, you have your funny pants on, do you?" I paused, then gave him the I'm-serious stare. "Do you want me to get a cot, or do you want time alone?"

"I'm good either way," he said, his eyes returning to the football game.

"Please just give me a preference."

"You decide."

"I want to stay here, but I'm worried about Westy."

"You know what, you go home, give Westy a walk. It'll be good for both of you. Just promise to come back tomorrow."

"I don't want to leave you." A wave of nausea mixed with sorrow washed over me like a rogue wave in the sea. "I can have my sister go over and stay at our house."

"She's probably on a date or something. So get Westy her dinner and relax. I'm tired anyway. We have a big day of testing tomorrow. And, you know, you already have a ninety-pound German shepherd who is going to bark you the riot act." He laughed, eyes still glued to the screen.

"Who are you rooting for in this game?" I asked, taking a break from our uncomfortable discussion.

"I'm not sure."

"Okay." I looked at the floor. "I just . . ." I was about to say "feel guilty," then realized that yet again I was making this about me, and it wasn't. "You know what? I got it. I'll call you when I get home." Leaning over, I kissed Luke and then walked out the door.

"Can you close the door, love?"

As soon as I did, tears streamed down my cheeks. My body felt paralyzed. The world was blurry as I slid down until the cold hard floor hit my butt.

Coming out of nowhere, Lara squatted next to me, wrapping her arms tightly around my shoulders and staying silent for a moment. "Maggie," she said softly, "I know this is hard. Do you have any questions?" I shook my head, grabbing a tissue she offered. "Tonight is probably going to feel surreal. If you want to stay here, we can get you a cot, but if you need to go home and take care of yourself, you should do that. Just try to breathe. Be patient with yourself. You have a lot of new information to absorb. It takes time."

"I came in today with a healthy husband and a dream of a fiftieth wedding anniversary, and now, only hours later, I'm leaving not knowing if my husband is going to die this week."

Lara helped me stand. My knees were weak and shaky. She held me up until I got my footing, but she didn't let go. She embraced me on our whole walk down the hallway, then turned and pulled me in for a hug. My head rested on her shoulder, which became soaked with my uncontrollable sobs.

Taking a deep breath, I took a step back. "I gotta go. I have a large dog at home who needs her dinner. I can't disappoint her." Westy always grumbled and barked until I set her dish on the floor. Undoubtedly, she was already ramping up her routine for my arrival home at this late hour. That was normal. Normal sounded so good.

Lara handed me a business card with a phone number. "This number goes to the nurses on this floor twenty-four hours a day, seven days a week. Use it day or night. Any questions?"

I pushed the elevator button. "I think I got it."

"Why did you guys name your German shepherd dog 'Westy'?"

I paused and thought for a moment, my focus shifting. A grin spread across my face. "Westy is a barrel-chested, moody dog who has a desperate need for men to love her. So we named her Mae West, or Westy for short, after the old silent-picture star." The elevator arrived.

"I love it! Try to get some rest, and I will see you soon." She waved.

I smiled at her gratefully as the door closed on this first experience in Oncology.

4

THE MINUTE MY CAR PULLED INTO THE DRIVEWAY, Westy's dinner demands were clear, even through the locked door. The armfuls of hospital paperwork made me move slower, and the barks became more desperate.

With the click of the lock, I heard the clack of her giant paws rushing to the entryway. My big black-and-tan furball bounced, blocking my way. Pushing past her, I dropped the contents of my arms onto the recliner closest to the door as she licked any piece of me she could reach.

"Oh, Westy, you must have a doctorate in dog-in-the-way-ness. If you want your dinner, you gotta move!" Patting her soft fur gave me comfort. It was such a familiar texture signifying home and love.

Once in the kitchen, she stopped barking and sniffed me as if her goal was to inhale the clothing right off my body. Did she know what was happening? Could she sense the hospital? Did she know it was a scary place?

As she calmed, her large brown eyes looked up at me, and her tail began to wag. She curled her body around my legs, getting close enough for more pets. I rubbed her ears, chest, and back, scratching right above her tail. After a few minutes, she ran to the front of the house, peering out the window looking for Luke. My heart sank. When she didn't see him, she went back to work, checking out my pants and shoes.

"Are you hungry?" Her head snapped up. She grabbed her favorite green duck toy that used to squeak and threw it around in celebration as I put the food in her bowl.

"Sit." She reluctantly did a half sit. "Westy? Come on, sit down." Her butt sank to the floor. "Madame, tonight we will be serving a nice venison crunch topped with some fresh chicken from last night's dinner. Does this meet your approval, my fine friend?" She remained seated, but her tail swept the floor with fast broad wags and her front paws danced with excitement. "What do you say?" She let out a tiny bark that sounded like she was whispering the word *woof.* I loved this daily, ordinary routine.

Westy stuffed her furry face into the bowl once it hit the ground, only pausing for brief moments of *crunch, crunch, crunch*. With the additional chicken, it took her an extra thirty seconds to lick all the sides of the bowl to ensure no morsel went uneaten. Watching her eat gave me some peace.

When Westy arrived at our house, a scared two-year-old rescue, we noticed right away she had trouble sitting. We tried to check under her tail, but she would not let us touch her backside. After she had been in our family for two days, we finally tag-teamed and succeeded in Operation Look Under Her Tail. There we saw a tumor sticking out from her bottom. Finally, we'd found what was hurting her. Staring at this mass, my mind had raced. Was this cancer? Was she going to die? My clammy hands had reached for her fur, and I'd begun to cry. Luke had stood still, likely frozen in fear until Westy licked each of us and broke the spell.

Within two days, we got her into the vet and had it removed, along with a rotting tooth. She quickly gained more energy. For the first time, we saw her play with toys. We were hopeful and terrified at the same time. Then came a call from the vet. Westy's tumor was not cancerous. Luke and I had cried with joy. Our new dog was cancer-free.

Once she recovered from her surgeries, we set to work, trying to overcome the abuse she suffered in her first two years. We didn't know the details, but she was afraid of shoes, strangers, and any loud noise, including the sound of a cup being placed on a table. Westy slowly relaxed. Now, four years into our relationship, Westy knew she was safe. We'd taught her to sit for her food, shake, and even give quiet and silent barks. Luke and I were proud. We made an excellent team.

My vision began to blur, and tears stung my eyes with the memory. I missed Luke. Everything in our previously warm home felt so empty without him. Wetness covered my flushed cheeks. Movement became necessary to avoid getting stuck staring into space.

The shower beckoned. Hoping to wash all traces of the hospital and pain off myself, I scrubbed my hair. As the hot water ran over me, I could briefly forget what the day had brought. Westy sat on the mat outside the shower.

Phoning Luke was next on my list.

"Hello," his groggy voice answered.

"Hi, sir, do you know anyone who has a bad monkey?" In the background, Westy went into a frenzy, trying to find her toy.

"Oh . . . that bad monkey," he said, chuckling.

Westy found her toy and began parading around the house, swinging it from side to side.

"Let me guess. She's tossing it around?"

"You got it!" My smile started to fade. "So, how are you feeling?"

"Like it's time to take Westy for a jog. I'll be home in ten."

"Ha, ha, mister. What's the truth?" Westy stopped barking and watched me pace the living room.

"I'm fine. You know how many people here are doting on me. They keep offering food, drinks, snacks, and drugs. I'd say I've landed myself at a fancy resort where I am the king. You remember that."

"I'm jealous. Maybe I need to come back and protect you from the hordes of admirers?"

"Nah, get some sleep. I'm gonna pass out here soon. They gave me some melatonin. It should do the trick."

"Rest up, and I'll be there before you wake up."

With that, he broke into laughter. "If you get here before I wake up, I'll know someone kidnapped my wife!"

"Okay, so I'll be there about four hours after you wake up."

"Now that sounds more like it! Love you, hon." Luke chuckled.

"Ditto, ditto, beep!" I said, our code for "I love you too."

Westy watched me slowly curl into a ball on one side of our oversized brown leather couch. My sobs mounted so quickly that it was nearly impossible to catch my breath.

Westy rose from her bed and sauntered over to me. She stared, panting for a moment before resting her big, soft head in my lap. Petting her head consoled me for well over an hour. She never moved or even fidgeted. She just held her space, letting me know she was there. It was unwavering love, the kind of love Luke deserved. Tomorrow I would hold this space for him while he went through all the tests.

THE BANGING ON THE DOOR and Westy's fierce barking woke me with a start. My heart began pounding out of my chest.

Grabbing my phone, I hit the app for the outdoor security cameras Luke had installed only a month ago. As the banging continued and the image of the porch slowly loaded, I slid down behind the couch, hoping it would hide me from the small leaded window. I shook my phone, willing it to load faster, my eyes darting between the door, Westy, and the blurry image. My house could have been robbed by now. Why does technology load so slowly when you need it most?

Then Westy exchanged the barking for excitedly jumping all over the place. Finally, in the window, a face appeared. My sister, Ronnie, peered inside through cupped hands.

"Get your lazy ass to the door, Mags!"

Westy ran around grabbing different toys, deciding what to present to the known cookie-giver when she entered.

The clock showed one o'clock in the morning. So what the hell was she doing here? Westy's bouncing made getting to the door tricky.

"Mags, get your ass to the"—the door swung open—"Good god, woman, what the hell happened to you?" She snapped her gum. "Were you preparing for a drag-queen-in-misery contest, or have you just stopped trying to look decent?" She pushed past me and headed into the kitchen, Westy following behind. The fridge door clicked. She popped the cork out of a wine bottle and poured herself a glass.

"You want one?" she yelled from the kitchen. Westy's paws danced on the tile floor. They were both just out of view from my spot on the couch. Next came the clink of the cookie jar lid and a satisfying crunch as Westy devoured her cookie.

After a moment, after not receiving an answer, Ronnie appeared in the living room where I had curled back up on the couch. "What? Are you giving me the silent treatment for showing up so late, or early as the case may be?" She gulped about half of her full wine glass. "Don't you want to know why I'm here?"

"Yup."

"Well, it doesn't seem like it."

"Super curious." I wasn't ready to talk about Luke. If Ronnie were a regular sympathetic sister, I could have recounted our day today, but this was not the case. Ronnie was not exactly the best support system for emotional times. She never had been.

For example, I had really needed her during my sophomore year in high school. I'd spent that year pining after a cute junior with big brown eyes and two deep dimples. His name was Brock. When he approached me at lunch and asked me to the winter dance, I was elated and nearly screamed yes in the middle of the cafeteria. My friend Julie had to pull on the back of my shirt to remind me to play it cool.

From that point on, he and I were inseparable for almost two months. His parents even asked me to join their Sun Valley ski trip for spring break. Then, just as fast as it had begun, he approached me during one of the rare lunch periods when we didn't eat together. He tapped me on the shoulder and said, "You're dumped. I'm with Allie now." I stared after him as he walked away and joined Allie at the cheerleaders' table.

When I got home from school, I'd found Ronnie reading *Sense and Sensibility* on the couch. I fell into her lap, knocking the book onto the floor, and relayed what had happened before making a sobbing, snotty mess on her shirt. When my sobs finally slowed, she chuckled and said, "Pull it together there, sissy. It was just a month! Try being dumped after going out for a year!"

I'd sat there stunned for the second time that day. Ronnie shared no comfort for me, then or now.

Ronnie chugged the second half of her wine. "Remember Devan, that hot Jamaican guy I dated for about six months?" She paused, staring at me intently, drawing out the drama as much as possible. I didn't answer. "You look like hell. Can you go clean your face? Then, and only then, I'll tell you my news. You look like a band member from Kiss."

"Ronnie, come on. It's one o'clock in the fucking morning. Of course I look like crap. Just spill it."

"Nope, you clean up. I'll grab another glass of wine."

With that, she jumped to her feet and headed to my refrigerator. Westy followed, hoping for another treat.

Relaxing on the couch was all I wanted to do. But I knew from experience that Ronnie would continue to hurl insults and finish all the wine in my house unless I gave way. An image of Luke sitting in bed alone at the hospital entered my mind. Could he sleep, or was he lying there scared, awake, and alone? Calling him right now was not an option. Not only should he be allowed to sleep, but Ronnie couldn't know what was going on yet. Maybe a text would be okay? But first Ronnie had to go. I complied with her demands and made my way to the bathroom.

Greasy black mascara was smeared down my cheeks and my bloodshot eyes looked atrocious. I wondered why my appearance had not inspired further questions, even from someone as self-centered as my older sister.

"Are you done yet? This is such amazing news." When I returned, she said, "Oh, thank god. Now you look somewhat normal."

"What, Ronnie? What is it?"

"Devan just got signed to be the male face of Guess AND *People Magazine* named him this year's Sexiest Man Alive." She flipped her shiny black hair over her shoulder. "I regret breaking his heart. Oh, that gorgeous smooth dark skin and those sparkling, mysterious eyes.

I should call him." She took another gulp of wine. "I, officially and most literally, dated the hottest man on earth! I'll bet he wants me back." She kicked her feet onto the ottoman revealing long, tanned legs stretching out from her tiny miniskirt.

I rolled my eyes. "Is this what you needed to tell me at one o'clock in the morning?"

"Um, wouldn't you want me to know if Luke was declared the hottest man on earth?" she asked in a serious tone. "I know I'm always the one with all the gorgeous men, but if it were you, you'd want me to drool and congratulate you!"

"I would have waited for you to be awake. Like, in the morning." Standing up, I hoped this would cue her to leave.

"Hey, jealousy," she said with a grin, snuggling deeper into her seat. "Lukie! Luke, Luke, Luke, get out here! You are missing amazing news!" she yelled, ignoring me as I shook my head. "Oh, relax! You know he is going to be impressed with your hot sister winning the heart of the world's most desirable man."

Of course, she wanted his attention. Luke always humored my sister because he found her stories entertaining despite the annoyance of her bragging. Plus, he loved to egg her on and make her stories grow as she told them. Without him, all the fun seemed gone. Even Westy had resigned herself to the floor and began to snore.

"Luke isn't here tonight. It's just me." I grabbed her glass. She swiped at me to get it back. "It's time for bed. Let me drive you home. You can come back to grab your car in the morning." She tried to fight me but fell back into her chair.

"Fine, Little Miss Priss. I don't want to fight." She wobbled to my car, complaining the whole way.

5

THREE HOURS AFTER DROPPING MY DRUNK SISTER OFF at her house, I woke up feeling across the bed for Luke. For us, most mornings started with me rubbing his back. My phone showed me it was only five thirty in the morning. What the hell was I doing up? And where was Luke? Wiping the crust from my eyes clarified the empty bed next to me. My ears perked up for any sign of life in the house. If Luke were home, he'd be in the next room watching TV. The silence was deafening. I couldn't smell coffee brewing either. Reaching over to his side of the bed, my hands felt the sheets. Cold.

My detective routine continued as I ran into the living room and crashed through the kitchen, den, bathroom, and mudroom. Where was Luke? I could see his silver car nestled into its spot outside the front window. I stood in the middle of our living room, motionless.

The room started to spin. My stomach dropped. I felt light-headed. Cancer. I took a few steps, then fell to the floor. It took me a moment before I realized I was screaming. How long had it been?

My throat was sore and dry. Westy ran to me. She licked my face and then lay down, wrapping her warm fur around me as I curled up.

We stayed that way for a short while until I realized I needed my phone to send Luke a text.

Good morning, honey. I hope I'm not waking you. I sat back down on the floor. Westy snuggled in.

I stared at my phone. Maybe I was wrong. Could it have been a bad dream? Hopefully, in a moment he'd write, *Boys' trip is off to a great start. We just got to California. The weather is gorgeous. We'll take our cars out on the track tomorrow.*

Last night at the hospital, a drunk Ronnie—that could have been a nightmare.

My phone buzzed with a new text.

What have you done with my wife? She would never get up this early. Did you sleep okay?

No words came. Westy licked my hands repeatedly, sensing my upset. It was no use. This was real. My hands shook.

I slept okay . . . after Ronnie left. I think she cleared out our wine rack.

LOL. And I was hoping you'd bring booze just to help me with this day of testing. How is Ronnie?

His hearty laugh rang in my ears, almost as if he were home. How was he so calm?

His voice was the only thing that would help bring me back to earth. But dialing the phone with my trembling hand was brutal.

"Well, hello, sexy!" he said. "What made you use that contraption to transmit your voice?"

My nerves settled. "Ha, ha! It's just easier sometimes. Can I come over now? Want anything?"

"Finally, you see things my way and can use the phone to talk. This is a miracle!" he teased. "They brought me a fantastic breakfast burrito this morning. Not as good as yours, though. The coffee was small. Bring me a drip, please?"

"You bet, love."

"You may want a book or something. I'll be in and out of testing all day. First, they gotta find out what this alien in my chest is up to. He sure is making it hard to breathe."

"Bad night?" I cringed.

"Don't get too jealous, but let's just say I got to know my nurses pretty well."

I sighed. *I should have been there.*

Like always, it was as if he heard my thoughts. "Ah, it's fine. The beds prop up, and that helps a ton. Don't you worry. They will figure it out soon, and we will be back to normal in no time. I miss my dog. Give Westy loves for me?"

"Of course! I'll drop her off with the neighbors and head in your direction."

"Why not leave her with Ronnie?"

"I don't trust her to take care of herself, much less Westy for a whole day. She'd probably just put leftovers on the floor and call it good." My laugh sounded forced. "I'll get Westy sorted, grab some coffee, and see you in about forty-five minutes. That good?"

"Yes, as long as you come bearing a new episode of the Ron-Dramedy."

"I got a good one for you."

WALKING DOWN THE ONCOLOGY HALLWAY less than an hour later, I was unable to stop myself from peering into patients' rooms—most of which contained older people without much hair sleeping and looking very sick.

Is this where Luke would end up? Would he soon lie nearly motionless with a gray pallor to his skin?

My pace sped up, as if by walking quickly I could remove this option from our path. I was briskly moving along until one room caught my attention. A moment of deep tenderness between the two people inside gripped my heart. A bald woman in her late fifties lay sleeping. Next to her was a very young woman with long curly hair, holding the older woman's hand and resting her head on the bed. Then she sat up and gently caressed the older woman's face. Was this her mother? A vision of my own mother on life support years ago flashed through my head. I'd held her hand, tears streaming down my face until Ronnie appeared. She held my other hand until my grip loosened. I kissed my mother's face for the last time as the machines pumping air into her lungs loudly mirrored the thump in my heart.

The young woman started to turn her head to the doorway, shaking me out of my memory. My intrusion was embarrassing. This emotional moment was private.

This image of beautiful and terrifying love lingered in my mind, as did a heartache of my own. Luke was my everything. Did that young woman have hope for her patient months or even weeks ago? Now here she lay with her head on the bed, just waiting for change.

Stop, I told myself. *Positivity is the best way to be supportive today. In this time of uncertainty, the last thing Luke needs is negative energy, Maggie.* Outside the room and out of view, I jumped up in the air to restore my energy, a Tony Robbins tactic. The door creaked open.

"You gotta lube up," Luke said with a smirk, pointing to the hand sanitizer on the wall. "I've been waiting ALL morning to make just that joke. Now get over here and give me a smooch."

Within a few hours, Luke was rushed away for myriad tests. I kicked off my shoes and rested my feet on the edge of the mattress.

Then, as I grabbed *People Magazine*, my guilty pleasure, a wave of guilt washed over me. How could I relax here while he endured god only knows what?

Usually, this magazine took me out of my little world and transported me to the land of celebrity gossip. Who was dating whom? Which couples were divorcing? Who had gotten engaged? And my favorite: Who wore it best? Today, none of the images could hold my attention. My brain wandered quickly through memories and worries, jumbling the two into one.

My legs fidgeted, begging to move. A walk was clearly in order. I left the room and headed in the opposite direction of the room I'd passed earlier. Maybe the woman wouldn't recognize me, but who needed to risk that? As embarrassed as I was, I knew my eyes would not be able to resist my voyeuristic tendencies.

Pacing the figure-eight hallway of the cancer floor helped burn off some energy. After an hour of walking past the family lounge what seemed like a million times, it beckoned. Maybe there was some reading material there that could help us understand what our lives were about to become. Inside sat the young woman with long curly hair. She was quietly eating a bowl of soup while putting puzzle pieces together. My gaze landed on the wall of pamphlets. Out of the corner of my eye, I saw that she was looking at me and smiling. I turned my head and smiled back.

"I'm sorry I was so nosy, looking in on your room during such a personal time," I blurted out before I could put much thought into my words. "I'm Maggie, your local Peeping Tom."

"I'm Becca. It's impossible not to look in rooms. Don't worry about it. If I'm honest, I've peeked in yours too." We both laughed. "I don't want to overstep, but I saw you last night on your way out. Did you recently get the diagnosis?"

I fidgeted with my wedding ring. Becca moved over next to me.

"My mom got her diagnosis two years ago. It's been a lot to manage, but we're doing it. My dad doesn't have the heart to see her this sick. So I'm the main caregiver. Without these amazing doctors and nurses, I don't know what I'd do."

"Wow, two years? I'm less than twenty-four hours into this slog, and I'm already worn out."

"Yeah, it ebbs and flows. You'll find your emotions are all over the place."

"How do you handle your day-to-day life? Like the normal stuff?" I asked sheepishly.

"Well, I shower and change at my dad's house, which is where I live right now. I'm saving money so I can become an oncology nurse one day."

"Wow, now that's dedication. I can barely watch Luke go through this, much less see many other people struggle daily." I shook my head.

"Or you can see nursing as guiding people on their path and helping them wherever they are."

I laughed. "Or that."

"Not that I am in that mode all the time." She grinned. "Sometimes I want to drop to my knees and give God a piece of my mind. But that too passes, I find."

"I felt like I was losing it last night. One of the nurses ushered me to the elevator. She caught me falling apart outside my husband's door. How embarrassing."

"It's human to struggle watching someone you love suffer. In fact, experiences like that made me want to be an oncology nurse. My brother was here right after the diagnosis. He tried to be the big strong guy, but he lost it. They let him cry until he started to get loud and angry. Thankfully, they saw his Seahawks jersey and started to talk about football, using that subject to ground him. His torment wasn't over, but he got a bit of a break, which I think he needed. They didn't know this, but after sorrow often comes rage for my brother."

"Wow, so we're all in good hands. You're inspiring, Becca!"

She smiled. We continued to chat for about an hour. She told me about nursing school. What an angel she was, to experience this and still want to help others get through it. Running away would be my preferred action, but only with Luke by my side. So, for now, we'd do this reluctantly but together.

I looked at my watch and stood up. "I should probably go back and check in on Luke."

Becca nodded. "I'm sorry you both have to go through this journey. I don't wish it on anyone. If I may give you a few words of support? Don't lose sight of the man. People may start referring to him as a cancer patient, but he is and always will be your husband, and that will never change." She paused and handed me a tissue. "Ask questions, no matter how dumb you think they may sound. The only dumb question is the one unasked. Ask until you feel like you know your options. Lastly, don't forget to breathe. Sometimes that might seem like the only thing you have control over. I know you'll get through it."

"Thank you. May I hug you?"

She stood up and grabbed me tightly. Although she was a tiny woman, the warmth and kindness were nearly overwhelming.

A nurse arrived in the doorway as if on cue. "Luke is back in his room. The doctor is waiting to speak with you both, Maggie."

I was nervous. Could this be the diagnosis?

FOUR PEOPLE WERE STANDING AROUND LUKE'S BED. The sanitizing foam burned my hands a little as I rubbed it in.

"I'm Dr. Proctor," one said. "Yes, you can call me Doc Proc." He chuckled at his joke, and Luke followed along. Laughter for me, at this moment, was out of the question. I shifted my weight from foot to foot to burn my nervous energy.

"We have completed testing today. We'll be sending you guys home shortly and ask that you come back on Monday for a biopsy."

"Will I be checked back in on Monday?" Luke asked.

"No, we'll do the scan, then you can go home. We won't receive results for about four days after that. You can stay at home until we have found the best course of treatment."

"Great, thanks, Doc." Luke grinned. "Now, can I get outta here and go see my dog?"

Doc Proc laughed and signed orders for his release. After many handshakes, the group of medical professionals disappeared down the hallway. They were barely out of the room when Luke got busy packing.

"Let's get out of here," he said, walking out the door without waiting for a response. I followed, still speechless.

Once home, I ran next door to the neighbors to pick up Westy while Luke headed inside. When the neighbor opened the door, Westy barreled past me and into the house. She crashed through the door, and Luke's laughter streamed all the way outside. She was surely licking Luke's face, hands, and anything else she could reach. By the time I got into the house, she was past excitement and into serious sniff mode. Finally, she narrowed in on the middle of his chest and took a deep inhale.

"Westy, meet Arnie," Luke said. I had never thought about it until now, but she had sniffed around his chest a lot before we went to the hospital. Had she been smelling cancer and trying to clue us in on what was about to happen? I shuddered at the thought.

After Luke washed the hospital off himself, we settled in on the couch, staring at the 5:00 p.m. news without saying anything. When the news ended, we just rolled into the next show. Luke was likely fine with the quiet, but I wasn't. This felt so familiar and incredibly awkward all at the same time.

"You feeling kinda strange, honey?" I asked.

"For a guy with an alien growing in his chest, I feel pretty good." He smiled, then immediately turned his gaze back to the TV.

"Can we talk?"

"Sure," he said, turning to me. "What do you want to talk about?"

"Uh . . . what we went through in the last twenty-four hours. How are you feeling? What are you thinking? Did I do the right thing leaving you alone at the hospital?"

"I can't waste energy on worrying. So I've decided to follow the plan and wait for a full diagnosis. Are you okay with that?"

"Yeah, okay," I lied. I wanted to talk about it. But it also made sense that he didn't. He just wanted to return to normal. The silence was his way of coping. He was practical, waiting for information before winding himself up. This trait was one of the many things that made me fall in love with him, but now it was stressing me out.

He was right. What exactly was there to talk about? We'd likely just run over the terrible experience to date. I sat there worrying about worrying while he sat watching a *Jeopardy!* rerun and shouting answers at the screen. It was time to move again to avoid getting stuck. I needed a project that would help get my mind off cancer, fear, and the albatross of the unknown. The kitchen beckoned. I choose Cooking Thai Chili Enchiladas for 400, Alex.

6

MONDAY MORNING, I DESCENDED from my home office and fell onto the couch.

"That went better than I expected. Heroic Video is always good to us employees, but I'm in shock at this level of kindness. We don't even know what's going on yet. I just wanted to tell Marko why I may be in and out a lot more."

"What did he say?"

"They understand we are in limbo. Marko told me that family is the most important thing and offered me as much time off as I needed for now. So they are temporarily changing my position to be more sales- and blog-oriented so I can be with you as much as possible. Then we will come up with a long-term plan when we know what we are working with. How cool is that?"

"Okay . . . I guess," Luke said. He took a deep breath and settled back farther into the couch. "Don't jeopardize your career on my behalf. You worked hard to get there!"

I had worked hard to get there. In the early aughties, I was living in LA with a dream of becoming a television producer. Through networking and good college connections, I found myself at Mark Burnett Productions just as they launched *Survivor*. For ten years, working endlessly helped me climb the ladder of reality TV and make it to supervising producer by the time I was thirty. Finally, after finishing an awful show based in a brothel, I'd had enough. I dropped my life in LA and moved back home to Seattle and in with my parents.

Starting over in Seattle was tough. There wasn't much reality TV work in Seattle, so bringing life to corporate video became my job. It took me nearly a year, but a production company that supported Microsoft, Starbucks, and a few other companies snapped me up. At first, I was assigned all the projects no one wanted, mainly because the client was mean. One we called the "Friday Night Screamer," so named because he would call nearly every Friday and yell at his producer without fail. Once I was on to his tirade pattern, my voice mail got to deal with the slurs and name-calling. Every Saturday, I called him back, and he'd act as if nothing had happened. In the end, he loved me and the projects, so he kept requesting me. This dedicated client helped me build a reputation in Seattle. When that agency closed, Heroic Video offered me a position running a talk show for Microsoft. That was an opportunity I couldn't pass up.

Three years later, my show was successful and a blast to work on. However, it did seem time to freshen it up and give it a new voice. How many episodes should one person write?

"I won't lose anything," I assured Luke.

"But what about *Innovations Today*?" he asked. "Won't you miss your show?"

"It's time to pass the baton. I'll meet with new clients and help them design campaigns to fit their brand. That sounds exciting, too, doesn't it?"

"No, not to me. But it sounds like you like the idea."

"Yup! Speaking of which, I need to write up a plan for what I will do over the next few months. I'll come back downstairs around two, so we can head over to your biopsy."

"I can—"

"No, sir, I am going with you. Plus, they said they would shove a giant needle through your chest. Maybe you won't want to drive after that?"

"As you wish." He grinned.

I loved this man. He was the Westley to my Buttercup.

LUKE SIGNED IN AT THE HOSPITAL DESK. I sanitized my hands before finding a seat. Then, as I took a sip of coffee from my travel mug, it went down the wrong pipe. I began to cough and gasp.

"Excuse me, ma'am," the receptionist yelled, "if you are sick, you cannot be here."

I gasped to catch my breath. "Wrong pipe," I called back, holding up my coffee.

Luke began to laugh. "She does that all the time." I continued to cough as quietly as possible as the other patients around me stared. Finally, some got up and moved to seats farther away from me. I threw my coffee away.

Anytime I'm stressed, I play a silly mobile game called Bubble Popper. It's mindless, but it calms me down. When Luke joined me, he reached over and popped some of the bubbles on my screen.

"Shit, you ruined my strategy."

"You ruined mine with your gagging routine."

"Fair enough." Reaching around, I rubbed his back. He leaned forward, giving me more space to do so.

"Luke," they called out a few minutes later, and we both stood.

"May I join?" I asked.

"I'm sorry you can't. The main waiting room has a screen showing your patient's status. Please wait there. We will call you over the system once he's ready to be taken home. It should be about one hour."

We kissed. Luke walked back behind the door. I grabbed my backpack and went to the waiting room. There they had a ton of large screens with names on them. I saw that Luke was in prep for the procedure. The corner of the room had tiny desks with power outlets. The workspace was perfect. My *Innovations Today* script needed help before it got passed on to the next producer to make it their own.

Working on my script and reviewing emails kept me busy for the next hour. The team at Heroic had made an announcement about Luke's cancer at our Monday meeting. Now, well-wishers were filling my inbox with offers to help ease my workload. Gratitude overtook me with each email *bing*, a helpful distraction from overthinking the needle being jammed into my husband's chest.

Every ten minutes, the statuses for all the tests would change on the screen. It had changed from "Pre-operation" to "Operation" for Luke and was now "In Recovery." Once his procedure was over, I relaxed a bit, perking up each time an announcement blared through the waiting room. Each of us in the room would stop and listen intently, then sigh almost in unison if it wasn't about our person. After an hour, worry overtook my focus. Checking and rechecking the board was my main activity. Finally, I went to the front desk, and the man there told me that he'd call me when my husband was ready. Terror struck. Had something gone wrong?

I tapped my pen on my notebook, creating a black cloud representing the fears floating through my brain. After another half hour, the man told me to wait again. I sat back down. Another half hour went by and the man making the announcements still did not call out Luke's name. The man behind the desk finally went on a break, and a new person took his spot. I rushed to the desk in mere seconds. I told the woman my story and how long it had been. She asked me to wait for a second and made a few calls.

"Oh dear, they have been trying to reach you. You're in the wrong waiting room. The screens have all the patients on it, but the waiting room for you is up that hallway, make a left, then another left."

She had barely finished speaking before I hurried to a small waiting room filled with anxious loved ones. There was no reception desk there, just a closed door. Rattling the door frantically made me more anxious. Even though the noise was loud, everyone seemed to ignore the woman shaking the door with all her might. Stopping for a second, I noticed an old-school telephone hanging on the wall. The handset pressed to my ear, I spoke so fast my breath ran out.

"Calm down, miss. I'll be out to get you in a moment."

A few minutes later, we were on our way to Luke's bed. I pulled the curtain back, and he was fully dressed.

"What took you so long?" he slurred.

"You have no idea." I wiped the sweat from my brow. "How are you feeling?"

He held up his cranberry juice box. "Fantastic. Can I get out of here?"

"If you can stand up, I will get the orders to release you," the nurse replied from behind me.

He gave her the thumbs-up and went to stand. He grabbed me as he nearly fell but quickly regained his balance and smiled.

"You best wait a bit more."

Luke lay back down. He slurped his multiple juice boxes for another five minutes, then tried standing again. This time, he was mostly steady.

"Looks like you are good to go. I'll get a wheelchair and bring you to your car."

"I can walk." He strutted about three feet forward, then walked the same distance backward.

"Hospital rules. You must go in a wheelchair."

Luke's nose crumpled with annoyance, but I knew he'd follow the rules. He did.

Bringing the car around, I saw Luke laughing with the nurse. They patiently waited for me to pull up. Finally, she helped me get Luke into the vehicle.

Once he was in, the nurse left, and I went to grab my sunglasses. They weren't there. They were in my backpack.

"Oh shit, Luke, I need to leave you here for a moment. I left my backpack inside."

"Sure." Luke leaned back and fell asleep. I turned on the flashers and ran back through the hospital to get my computer and backpack.

Just inside the door, I tripped and landed flat on my face. My fall was a physical expression of how my world was trending down.

The surgery announcer rushed over to me and helped me up. "You okay, miss?"

My face turned red as I nodded.

"Okay, you be safe now."

Thankfully, my computer and other belongings were in my work corner where I'd left them. Relief washed over me. It hadn't been easy, but together we had made it through another day.

7

AT WORK THE NEXT DAY, a few colleagues came over to check in on me. One sat down and wanted "the whole scoop." I shared my story but was frustrated by those who made it feel like a gossip session. Were they going to meet up with their friends and talk about their poor colleague, the cancer patient's wife, as they drank their wine?

In a large meeting room at two o'clock, I passed my talk show to a talented co-worker. Even though I knew Jill was a fantastic choice and would do great things with the show, I felt sad. This project had been mine since its inception. Handing it over to someone else was like giving my baby away.

After offering my full support at the meeting, I went into the bathroom and cried. Was I losing everything already?

The mirror reflected a sad woman with tear-stained cheeks and running mascara, a stranger. I leaned in. Deep in my eyes, I saw my inner warrior, ready to come out and go to battle. Now was not the time to cry. It was time to fight—for my family, my husband's life, my sanity, and my career. The best thing for me to do was to suck it up and embrace the generous offer to work from a hospital room. With a deep breath, I marched into Marko's office.

"Maggie Byrne reporting for duty." I saluted him. He turned in his chair and smirked.

"Great! I'm going to be sending you the five leads that we haven't followed up on over the past few weeks. So you can take it from there."

"Do you want to be on any of the calls? How shall I update you?"

"I trust you. We'll do a weekly meeting, and you can update me then. Sound good?"

"Yup."

He turned back to his computer. I started to leave, and he called out to me. "If you need more time or to take a break, let me know. Don't be afraid to ask." His tone showed compassion with every word.

"Work is going to be my sanity. So I need to continue being useful."

"Taking care of your husband is useful, I'd say."

"Yeah, yeah, yeah. I know." I shook my head at him and went back to my desk.

THAT NIGHT, Luke and I both crashed into bed, falling directly into a snoring competition. Luke's snore had an additional wheeze to it. He began to toss and turn. I turned on a light to see what was happening on his half of the bed.

"I can't breathe." He piled pillows under his head and back to prop himself up.

"That helping?"

"A little."

I rushed to the cabinet to grab more pillows. At this point, Luke was sitting so far up he might as well have been on a chair. Finally, he seemed to fall back to sleep. I watched him struggle to breathe. Occasionally he'd choke or gasp and I'd try to shift him to one side or the other.

"You awake?" I asked.

"Nope," he replied, beginning to cough.

"Not funny. We need to get you back to the hospital. You sound terrible."

"I'm not going back there until I have to. Just go back to sleep. I'll be fine."

"I'm not going to lose my husband, you hear me. We need to go now," I said in my sternest voice.

He began gasping for air. I jumped up and threw on my shoes. "Now. Let's go."

Standing up, he caught his breath again. "Let's call first thing in the morning. That sound like a deal?"

"You can't breathe!"

"We've only got four hours left. We'll call first thing in the morning. Just get some rest. I'll sleep out here in a chair."

I went back to bed, leaving our bedroom door open so I could hear him in the living room next door. After a bit, his snoring hit a pattern, and I snuck out to check on him. Sitting on the chair across the room, I watched and silently cried.

AT EIGHT O'CLOCK SHARP, I had Doc Proc, Luke's oncologist, on the phone. I explained how his breathing was impaired.

"Mmm hmm . . . I understand . . . No, he won't . . . Thank you." Luke's face went pale as he listened to me. "Can you call ahead? Two hours? We'll be there."

I hung up and turned to my husband. "Pack an overnight bag. We'll check in at the hospital and get a room upstairs again. Doc Proc said it would likely be a longer stay this time. Results aren't in yet, but he expects them in the next day or so."

Yoga pants, bras, socks, and slip-on shoes got tossed in a bag. Luke was looking through his clothing, trying to find the most comfortable things he owned.

"Did you tell him I refused to go in last night?"

I nodded, continuing to pack to distract myself from the fury coming from Luke.

"Why?"

"This isn't a betrayal. I said it because it's true. You did. I was terrified all night and didn't sleep. You looked and sounded miserable. Admit it! We have to come up with a way to handle this."

"It's no big deal. I did fine in that chair."

"Just stop it! I know you don't feel well, and I'm terrified. Your blasé attitude is not helping one bit."

He started to gasp again. I patted his back. Catching his breath, he took my face in his hands and gently kissed me.

"I'm sorry you have to go through this," he said, brushing a stray hair out of my face.

"I'm sorry, too, for both of us."

8

LUKE AND I SETTLED INTO A NEW ROOM just two doors down from where we had stayed over the weekend. Once Luke was admitted, the nurse came in with a round of questions that took about half an hour to answer. After that, we waited for Doc Proc to check in on us.

After watching an episode of *Let's Make a Deal* and *The Price is Right*, the door opened. A handsome young man appeared in our room. He said a quick hello, then walked over and buried his nose in the computer for a few moments before turning to us.

"Hello, I'm Dr. Woo. I wanted to see how you are feeling."

"I'm feeling okay. But it's pretty hard to breathe," Luke confessed.

"Do we know what kind of cancer he has yet? What is the prognosis? How long will it be hard to breathe? Is there a tumor in his lung?" I asked.

Luke laid his hand on my arm and shook his head. I knew that I could be overwhelming sometimes, but not knowing the chances of keeping my Luke alive drove me mad.

"You don't know your results yet?" Dr. Woo asked, turning to the computer, then back to us. "Diffuse large B-cell lymphoma."

"What's next? What's the prognosis?"

"I wish I could tell you, but I can't. Dr. Proctor will have to give that information when he arrives."

"When will that be?"

"By the end of the day."

My stomach dropped. I began to panic. Dr. Woo turned to Luke and performed a physical check with his stethoscope. Everyone was acting like this was normal. This was not normal.

"I'll be right back." I bolted out of the room, tears streaming down my face. I sat down on the couch in the family lobby, face in hands.

A hand gently landed on my shoulder. "Are you okay?" Becca stood over me. When I looked up, she sat down.

I shook my head, unable to speak.

"It's pretty hard, to be honest. I'm not sure what is happening right now but let it out. Feel free to emote in any way that relieves the pressure. I think I spent the first year of my mom's treatments crying in this room."

"We know he has cancer, but we don't know anything else about it. I just need to know," I choked out between my sobs.

"Not knowing is hard. But may I offer you a piece of advice that someone gave to me when I started this journey?"

I wiped at my nose with my sleeve like a belligerent child.

"There will always be things you don't know. So take it one moment at a time and focus on what is in front of you."

I looked up at her and smiled. I wiped my face with a new tissue. "You are something, Becca. How did you become so stoic?"

"I've been doing this for two years. I think the only thing I could do was accept it or go crazy. I'm still sad a lot of the time, though."

I leaned over and embraced her. "How is your mom doing?"

"The same. I do have hope. They just started her on a new trial. It could help. Right now, my mom is sleeping a lot and in a good deal of pain, but she's managing. I think she doesn't let on how bad it is sometimes because she's more worried about me than herself. I just wish my dad would help more. But he's just not willing to."

"That sucks," I said. "Sorry, that wasn't nice."

She laughed. "My dad isn't nice. So, no, it's okay. He's too selfish to help take care of his wife of nearly thirty years. I see you in here with Luke and I'm inspired. When I pick a partner, I'll keep that in mind—someone who will truly be there with me in sickness and in health."

"I hope for that too. How old are you, if I may ask?"

"Nineteen."

"You amaze me, Becca. Truly, you do." I smiled.

Becca got up. "I'm going to check on my mom. We're just over there if you want to talk. I'm here."

"Thank you," I said and watched her disappear.

ALL AFTERNOON, doctors and nurses were in and out of Luke's room. We may have had ten minutes alone throughout the whole day. Luke fell asleep, dressed in his street clothes and propped upright with a stack of towels.

Finally, around five o'clock, Doc Proc appeared. I woke Luke.

"Sorry it took me so long to get to you. We had a few emergencies pop up." Doc Proc sat down. I held my breath. "Luke has a six-inch tumor in his chest. The tumor is non-Hodgkin's large B-cell lymphoma. The tumor irritates your lungs, which is why the pleura is filling with liquid. There seems to be a small amount of fluid around your heart—"

"And the prognosis?" I asked before he finished speaking.

"Luckily, Luke is young and strong. This kind of tumor is inoperable, so we need to treat it with chemo. Before we do that, we need to do a PET scan to get a full picture. We need to see if there are other tumors. We also need to check your bone marrow to see if the cancer has spread there. Then we can decide on the right course of action."

My heart sank.

"When can we get this started?" Luke asked.

"Tomorrow, we can get you in for the PET scan. You will need to adhere to a no-sugar, no-carb diet for twenty-four hours before the test. The PET scan works because cancer feeds on sugar. First, we starve your body of sugars, then we give you a sugary drink before the scan. Cancer eats up all the sugar, and we make it glow."

"What about my marrow?"

"We will need to do a spinal tap. I'm going to try to get that in on Thursday. Today, we will drain your lungs again, then let you rest up."

Fifteen minutes later, Doc Proc returned with his tools for the lung draining. I left the room; watching them stick that large needle into Luke's back was too painful to watch. Instead, I walked the halls, peeking into rooms, wondering which room most closely represented the kind of journey we were about to go on. Finally, it was time to bite the bullet and call his mom.

LUKE'S FOLKS ARE LOVELY PEOPLE and usually calm. But, unfortunately, his dad Harlan's medical condition had them locked down in Australia, so I wasn't sure how this might affect them. My watch said it was five at night; that's nine in the morning in Perth. It was time. I dialed, knowing a grenade was about to be launched into their morning coffee ritual.

"Hello, Judy."

"Oh, hello, dear. How are you guys doing? We were just looking at Tappy and Trixie, wondering how our human kids are." At the mention of her dachshunds' names, a scuffle of paws exploded in the background. Then there was a giggle, likely from Harlan.

"I have news for you—"

Before I could finish, a squeal burst out on the other end of the line. "Honey! Are you pregnant? When you both crossed forty years old, we gave up on having grandchildren. But you've done it! This is fantastic."

"No!" I screamed, shutting her up right away.

"I'm sorry, darling. I just got excited. Then what is the news? I'm listening."

My heart hurt for her. Instead of telling a mother that she was gaining a family member, I was about to reveal that she could lose her only child. Tears streamed down my face. How many more were left at this point? The line was silent for a few moments while I wiped my face and sat up straight, regaining control.

"Are you okay, dear?"

"Luke has cancer," I blurted out, lacking an ounce of grace. "We are in the hospital getting tests to get further information. We don't know the treatment plan yet, but we should know by the end of the week."

"Oh, honey."

"I'm sorry, Mom. I hoped to be gentler, but it's just been hard."

"I understand. How is Luke handling this?" she asked calmly.

"He's in good spirits. Stoic like his normal self."

Walking through the last few days had been painful. Judy listened intently, whimpering quietly as each detail emerged. Of course, she asked if she should fly up but also mentioned her worry about Harlan's health. After discussing it, we decided she should stay put for now. She asked many supportive questions, told me she trusted us to make the best decisions, and offered to help any way she could, insisting that we call night or day. And she ended the conversation by saying that she was proud of us. Since my parents had passed years before Luke and I had met, Judy had become my mom too. I loved her dearly. Upon hanging up, a small amount of fog cleared. Her calmness alone had helped me find peace and hope, even though I'd dashed her wish for grandchildren all over again.

Guilt crept in, grabbing hold of my stomach and forcing my hands to shake. Walking calmed me down. As my loop around the oncology floor began, a beam of light came my way in the form of another patient. A petite Asian woman, dressed almost entirely in pink and dragging her chemo-drip holder around like an old friend, passed by me. Just seeing her on her walk made me smile. I waved and headed back to Luke's room.

I snuggled into the recliner and spent the next hour sending texts and making phone calls to friends and family members. The reactions to our news varied. In some cases, they were shocking. But who knows what to say when someone tells you your friend or family member has cancer? It's not an easy one. Many just apologized and offered help. Some started to cry and made it all about them: What would they do without Luke? Some told me stories of other people who died from cancer. There was even one person who told me not to get comfortable; even if it looked good, it probably wasn't. That was the last call I made. I needed a break. As I realized that everyone would also want updates, creating a cancer blog became a top priority. This way, friends and family could get up to speed without blowing up my phone.

I still had to call Ronnie, but I was fearful of how she'd respond. To avoid this dreaded task, another walk seemed in order. Since Luke was still sleeping, I left the twelfth floor and went outside to walk around under the trees and get some fresh air. Reflecting on the diagnosis brought little comfort, as did the feeling of being in limbo without a proper prognosis. What if our friend was right and we couldn't even trust a "good" prognosis, and Luke left us? With this thought, tears streamed down my cheeks again. Breathing deeply, I walked for another twenty minutes taking in the gorgeous pinks and purples of the sunset over the city.

When it was time to head back, my stomach knotted back up. Ronnie might handle Luke's news well, or she might blow up. When our parents had died, Ronnie had taken it upon herself to keep the house using the insurance money. I was seventeen, and she was twenty. She kept everything as normal as she could for me. She took on all the struggles to save me. Because of her, I didn't have to move to a new high school in the middle of my senior year. She helped with homework, paid for senior trips, managed the money, and kept a college fund for me to have the opportunities our parents wanted. Maybe Ronnie would turn into that big sister again, or perhaps she'd explode. I had no idea what to expect.

When I walked into the hospital room, Luke was awake and smiling. So instead of calling Ronnie, I climbed into his bed and curled up, cuddling the love of my life.

9

THE PRICE IS RIGHT played in the background while Doc Proc explained our next steps, turning the computer monitor with the results of the PET scan toward us. It showed a huge mass between the top of Luke's lungs, with a few smaller masses in various places all above his belly button.

Doc Proc talked to Luke about joining a new lymphoma trial they were doing. Luke agreed, and Doc Proc left for about five minutes. When he returned, he explained that we needed to start chemo immediately due to the tumor's urgent nature, placement, and size. Luke's treatment cycle would involve five days of full-time in-patient care on chemotherapy, then sixteen days at home. We would do the cycle six times.

"'Urgent nature,'" I repeated. "What does that mean? I thought we would get a second opinion from Seattle Cancer Care Alliance."

"Unfortunately, there's no time. We are worried that if we don't stop the mass from growing, it will close his esophagus and the surrounding vessels it is blocking. I recommend we start chemo today. I will let you two discuss it and make a decision, and I'll be back in a half hour."

Doc Proc left the room, and we looked at one another.

Luke grabbed my hand and kissed it gently.

"Off to the races we go. I don't see another option."

The room felt like it was closing in on me. It was hard to breathe. Beads of sweat popped up on my forehead and dripped down my face. I grabbed a tissue, wiping the perspiration away. The beeping coming from another room got louder. I tried to take a deep breath, inhaling the overwhelming scent of sanitizer.

I shook my head, and Luke went back to watching the goofy game show. The camera panned across an audience of colorful shirts, many featuring pictures of Drew Carey. He announced a name. The audience exploded into applause. The woman jumped up from her seat and danced her way down to her podium. I envied that woman, her carefree attitude as she was about to guess the price of soup. A simple task that could win her a great experience. I ached for that kind of simplicity so badly that my stomach cramped.

I turned to Luke, about to comment on how stupid the show was, but he was enjoying the break, chuckling at the spectacle. How did he always stay so stoic? He was about to be living in the hospital getting *large amounts of poisons* pumped directly into his veins, and he took this news as if they had just told him they were out of ham and cheese for lunch. I had more questions for him: Wasn't he worried? Didn't he want a second opinion? Did he just want to complain? I looked over as he laughed at the folks on TV arguing over how much a can of chicken noodle soup costs. No, he wasn't going to allow himself to stress. His choice was clear. Take the treatment here and now, or die.

"Are you okay, honey?" he asked me.

"Shouldn't I be asking you that?"

"No, we know I'm not okay. But you can be. Your forehead is pinched."

"I'm just worried."

He grabbed my hand and kissed it again. "I got this, babe."

"You don't know that. You really don't." I crawled up on his bed and placed my hands on both sides of his face. "You could get sicker and even die. It feels like you are not taking this seriously. If you die, I'm left alone without you. I don't want to be without you. I have no life without you. I love you, Luke, and this is not something to take lightly." I rested my head on his shoulder and sobbed. Luke petted my hair. I looked up. He had tears in his eyes too.

"Mags, we don't have a choice. Let's make the best of it. I'm scared too."

I grabbed him and squeezed him tightly into my chest.

"Ditto, ditto, beep," he whispered into my ear.

Treatment

10

ONCE WE AGREED TO THE TREATMENT, our room was swarming with nurses, doctors, and all kinds of specialists. Each person left pamphlets, notebooks, and advice. It felt like an open house where all the realtors stop to check the goods and drop off their cards. We were overwhelmed. Finally, it calmed down, and we had a moment alone. We just sat enjoying the quiet, looking out the window at the clear sky and city. It was gorgeous. Our silence was interrupted by a nurse who came to take him away to have his port installed.

As a nurse rolled Luke down the hallway, I watched the sun set over the city. I was so glad they were putting in the port, so he wouldn't have people stopping by to poke and prod him all hours of the day and night. Instead, they could simply go to the tube routed directly into his chest. However, convenience aside, the idea of putting a main line into your chest to supply a constant stream of poison sounded terrible. We were going to trust the medical staff. Then it dawned on me that we needed to be advocates for Luke's health.

The glow of my computer screen replaced the setting sun. Google popped up and I searched "large B-cell lymphoma."

My train of thought was interrupted by a loud throat clearing. Becca was standing in the doorway.

She asked me to go for a walk in the park that was a block away from the hospital. We walked in silence. I wondered if she needed me or if she knew I needed her. Finally, she sat down on the edge of a large fountain spraying mist all around us.

"The trial isn't working for my mom," she stated, sorrow covering her young face like a veil. "They have recommended we start to consider hospice. My dad is fighting me, insisting that she will get better if I give her more time. I finally stood my ground. I told him that she gave me power of attorney for a reason. He told me that if I killed her, he'd never speak to me again, and he hung up." She broke down into sobs. I rubbed her back and stayed silent.

I wanted to tell her it would all be okay, that her dad would come to his senses. But the truth was, I didn't know that. I hadn't even met the man, but he sounded difficult. I assumed he was often like this, given that his wife had put a nineteen-year-old woman in charge of her medical decisions, rather than leave that responsibility to her husband. Becca kept crying as we sat in silence, and I waited for her to continue.

When Ronnie decided to take our parents off life support after the crash, she hadn't even talked to me about this massive decision. She arranged the timing with the nurses, then took me to the hospital without one word about what was next. When we got to the room where both our parents lay, my world suddenly became so small. I stared at my mom and dad, unsure who to approach first. I chose my mother. I knelt by her side, begging her to come back. My sister rubbed my shoulders, pressing her cheek to the top of my head. After about an hour, she knelt next to me and encouraged me to kiss each of their faces before leaving. This should have been a clue that something was up. Later that night, she told me they were gone. Fury washed over me. Packing my bags, I screamed as loud as I could. I told her I hated her and slammed the door. For weeks, I stayed with my friend Julie, refusing to answer any of Ronnie's messages. Now I saw the torment and pain I had likely caused my sister. She had been trying to protect her immature teenage sister. I silently vowed to call her when I got back to Luke's room. Right now, I needed to focus on my friend in pain.

"Cancer sucks," I said, reaching out to squeeze her arm. "Know that you are smart and the decisions you make are the right ones. Your mother picked you for a reason. Do you think she wants to continue this way?"

"No. Yesterday my mom asked if we could move to Oregon for assisted suicide. If she wants that, she must be in unbearable pain." Becca looked up and choked out a laugh. "My mom was a nurse in a psychiatric institution for thirty years. She was stabbed, slapped, hit, kicked, and punched more times than I can remember. She'd come home from work with a black eye or some stitches and a smile. She'd tell me the story, highlighting how she could help this person. Never complaining. If you look at her right arm, you can still see a huge scar from where a patient cut her for giving him regular milk instead of chocolate."

"Wow, that's a brave woman."

"Yes, very brave. Let's change topics, please. How is Luke?"

Becca listened as I explained the situation. The worry that I couldn't get a second opinion weighed on me. She comforted me, telling me that Doc Proc came from Seattle Cancer Care Alliance. He was renowned for his treatment of lymphoma. If he said it was urgent to start chemotherapy, she believed him. We talked about work and school for a while before walking back to the oncology floor.

"One word of advice, Maggie. Whatever you do, avoid googling Luke's cancer. Websites make everything scarier."

11

ONCE THE PORT WAS IN LUKE'S CHEST, the nurses began the treatment. First up, steroid pills to counteract some of the side effects of chemotherapy and boost his energy. Once that was in his system, they connected him to his chemo cocktail.

Within minutes, Luke had jumped up out of bed and was cleaning the hospital room. He folded the extra sheets, stacked pillows, and started rearranging the furniture. A huge grin crept onto my face.

Luke is a neat freak. One of his mantras is "everything has a place, everything in its place." Seeing him fussing about to organize the small room felt familiar. It reminded me of when we had moved into our house. Before a single piece of furniture was allowed in the house, he measured and marked it out on the floor with painter's tape.

The day he laid out the plan for all our oversized furniture, I was at work. "Ta-da!" he said, proudly displaying his home layout work when I came in the door, tired from a long day on a shoot. He showed me a few options in the living room and bedroom, marked in two colors of painter's tape. Having the plan all sorted out was a treat.

I continued to smile at the memory while he finished moving his bed to the perfect spot centered on the wall. Then he sat on the edge, his eyes darting around the room, looking for something, anything, to keep his mind occupied.

"I feel buzzy. Those steroids make me feel anxious."

"Let's walk it off." I stood, moving to the door.

We walked in silence, him dragging the strange rolling contraption that held his chemo. Since he was going to be hooked up to this contraption twenty-four hours a day for five days straight, I figured this thing needed a name.

I jumped in front of Luke, starting to walk backward. "Hello, I'd like to introduce you to our new friend, Richard the chemo caddy. He's a real dick." We laughed at my dumb joke and continued our trip around the floor.

As we passed Becca's mother's room, I peeked in. They were both asleep. I'd catch up with her later.

After our walk, Luke lay back in his bed and turned on the news. I was starting to doze off when I heard the door fly open and hit the wall.

"Fuck you, Maggie. I mean, seriously. Why the hell did you tell everyone else, and I had to learn from Clarice?" Ronnie stormed across the room, glaring.

"Sorry, I was worried about your reaction, and I just wanted to find a good time to call."

"Right." She plopped into a folding chair and shifted her body to block me out. "How are you, Luke? I can't believe this has happened. What is that thing?"

Luke explained our next steps. She got up and kissed him on the forehead.

"I'm here if you need anything, Lukie." Then she abruptly turned to me. "As for you, miss, I don't want to speak to you. I can't believe you did this to me." With that, she flew back out the door, slamming it on her way out.

"Ronnie, stop!" I called down the hallway.

She turned on her heel. Her eyes were glowing with rage. "I have nothing to say to you."

"You realize, I'm dealing with a husband with cancer. This isn't about me. This isn't about you. This is about him. Luke. That guy in there we both love," I said, getting closer to her.

"I'm the one who has always been there for you. I should have been your first call. Not someone you didn't bother to call at all. You are an asshole."

I grabbed her arm and pulled her into the family lobby to prevent our voices from carrying into patient rooms. Thankfully, no one was in there.

"This is really hard, Ron. It's been crazy since last week."

"Last week?!? Have you known for a week? So you knew when I came over to your house, and you lied to me?"

"No, I did not lie to you. I just didn't tell you. I had only known for a few hours, Ron."

"That is the definition of a lie!" Ronnie pushed me aside and strode out of the room.

I flashed back to eighth grade. I had run for class president and Ronnie had helped me make some of my campaign signs. It was a significant boost to have my cool older sister showing support. I appreciated it so much. The day I lost the election, I came home and hid in my room. When she checked on me, I lied and told her it was a tie, and we needed a tiebreaker. Then I went to bed. Little did I know, Ronnie spent the night making more signs, all in multicolored glitter. The next day at school, there were at least ten signs in the entryway, all pushing people to vote for me in the tie. My classmates called me a sore loser and many referred to me as "Mad Maggie" or they would sing a variation on the Beck song "You're a loser, Maggie . . . why don't you kill us" as I walked the hallways. When I got home, Ronnie stood in the living room, arms crossed with traces of glitter on her usually meticulously clean face and hands. Turns out, the night before she had canceled a date with Jack, the new guy in the neighborhood that all the girls were dying to go out with, just to make and hang those signs. She yelled at me for an hour, then stormed out of the house. The silent treatment kept me on edge for nearly a month.

I walked back to Luke's room and sat down, my face in my hands.

"I didn't mean to hurt her, but I also didn't want to deal with this type of outburst right now."

"Or ever?" He winked. "You know she'll get over it in a day or so, right?"

"I hope so. Ronnie thinks I lied to her." My eyes darted around the room, looking for any distraction.

"Lied? How?"

"Because the night of our first trip to the ER, she came to our house, drunk, remember?"

"She wouldn't have been any help."

"I know that, and you know that. But Ronnie definitely doesn't know that." I wiped away a stray tear. "How is it you're always comforting me and not the other way around?"

"Oh, you just wait. I'm only starting this treatment. I bet I'll need a lot more help once this stuff starts its work." He grabbed the tubes and followed the line down to his chest. He examined it for a moment and began to futz with it. "I have an idea," he declared, eyes lighting up. Still in his street clothes, he routed the tube from his chest out between the buttons on his shirt and through the flap of the buttoned breast pocket to keep it from pulling. He smiled. "Ta-da." He held out his arms, showing me his handiwork. I got up and kissed him all over his face.

THE NEXT FEW DAYS AT THE HOSPITAL went by in a blur. I focused on work. I spent as much time as I could writing a few proposals for upcoming commercials and taking calls with clients and colleagues while Luke began to lose color and sleep a lot more. When he woke up with terrible nausea, which often happened, I'd get a cold cloth and wipe his face, holding the small, curved bucket under his mouth in case he got sick. Other times he'd wake up wanting to take a walk. I liked the walks.

A few days into his treatment, we ventured out for a hike around the circle, dragging Richard the chemo caddy behind. Down the hallway, we spotted a small woman in a black lacy sweatsuit with embroidered flowers on the sides of her arms and legs. As we got closer, I noticed a little purse over her arm, moving side to side as she walked. It was the smiling lady in pink I'd seen earlier in the week. I smiled, focusing on the bag. What would someone be carrying in there? She caught me staring and broke into a huge smile. She nodded to us as she passed.

"She moves really fast. I'll bet she's taking the chemo well." Luke grinned.

As we neared the lobby, we noticed a group of people standing together, crying. They were speaking to a younger man whose face seemed frozen in a sad expression. They would keep the children, they explained, while his wife got set up at home with hospice. Tears rolled down my cheeks as we passed. Luke looked straight ahead and moved quickly.

"Let's race," Luke said, clearly trying to distract me from staring. He took off, swiftly moving around the corner and out of view. I chased after him, only catching up past the threshold to the other half of the floor. "Beat ya," he said, tapping his foot on the shiny silver line that separated the two sides. We used the figure-eight-shaped floor as a track, ignoring the grim reality that one side was for blood cancer and the other side for non-blood cancers. Racing was always a good distraction.

I couldn't help but laugh. His smile was contagious.

"I didn't even try," I said, grateful for a moment of fun.

We headed back toward Luke's room, stopping in the hallway to look out over the city. Today, the sky was gray and the clouds ominous. Were they here to take the loved one from that family on which I had eavesdropped? Would these dark clouds come back to take my Luke?

Much of the crowd had cleared by the time we reached the lobby area again. Luke went into his room and quickly lay down, creating a loud creaking sound as he collapsed onto his bed. His eyes drooped with exhaustion.

"Want to watch *Jeopardy!*?" he asked. Before I could respond, Luke was snoring. Terrified, feeling alone, I tried to answer questions about Edgar Allan Poe. It was too hard to focus. Craving silence, I turned the TV off.

My mind continued to race. My gut hurt. I didn't want to be like that family in the hallway. I had an uncontrollable urge to sneak out and find the wife's room. With Luke safely asleep, maybe I could manage this without someone seeing me.

I crept down the hallway, pretending to be on a walk. I saw the young man enter a room near the family room, and I slowed down as I passed by. Inside lay a woman. She looked like she was young and had no hair. A large photograph sat on a table next to the bed showing a happy family. I slowed as I saw an additional lump on her bed, staring as I realized it was a second person. A man, likely her husband, was curled up on the bed like a small child.

Memories raced back to me. I had been driving home from my friend Veronica's house with Westy. A car began to swerve. I slowed. The driver was young, phone in hand. I stepped on the gas. A flash of the red car in my side mirror. The grind of crumpling metal. A fast-paced slide sideways. Westy tumbled into the back of the car. Which direction were we going? A high-pitched squeal. A scream, then black.

I came to in a smoke-filled car. Terrified we were on fire, I kicked to get free. Westy got into the front and licked my face. I kicked and kicked until someone opened the door and we escaped. Luckily, Westy and I had landed on all four wheels. The police, fire department, and EMTs arrived and checked us out. The world was hazy. Westy and I sat against the median on the side of the interstate. I didn't feel safe until Luke got there. He carefully transported us home, laid me in bed, and curled up next to me. "Don't ever scare me like that again," he said. "I can't lose you."

How many times had this man curled up on the bed next to this woman, praying she would survive? I imagined all the plans they had made together for their future and what they would do once she healed. Now he lay in that child-like position declaring his love and giving her permission to leave this earth, promising that he would keep her memory alive and their children safe.

Snapping back to reality, I realized that I was standing entirely still in their doorway. Lara, my favorite nurse, was standing by my side.

"Everything okay?" she asked, gently walking me away from the door. I shook my head. She wrapped her arm around me, allowing me to weep onto her shoulder as she guided me toward the room where my weak-looking husband slept.

Before she left, she offered me some cookies. It was tempting, but I had no appetite. I curled up on my chair and tried to flip through a *People Magazine*.

My head bobbed as tiredness overtook me. Images of the grim reaper floated through my head. I saw him haunting the hallway, looking for the woman only two rooms away. Being on the oncology floor wasn't some weird camp. It was real. Death haunted this floor, and we were here because Luke was under consideration for the taking. I awoke, sobs escaping my mouth.

Luke struggled, his tubes getting tangled, as he reached to comfort me for the second time today. He was getting weaker by the hour.

"The scary stories we keep hearing, we have to trust that's not us." He held me. I leaned closer into him.

"We don't know what will happen. So, it's about time we have a real conversation about what we do if we end up where that couple is right now."

Luke looked down at the ground and slowly sat back on the bed. "I can't think like that, Maggie. I just can't. I will beat this." He lay back and turned on the TV.

My face flushed with anger, which then subsided into sorrow. Luke was being brave and doing what he did best: taking care of me. I wondered how he was managing all the emotions he must be having.

12

LUKE FELT MORE AND MORE ILL as the chemo pulsed through his veins. He spent much of his time sleeping while I hustled for work meetings. The biggest project was a script for a new piece of technology that was so complex I had to do a ton of research to understand how it worked. Luckily, this research took so much of my brainpower that I'd lose hours of my day before returning to the reality of Luke sound asleep with a grayish tone to his skin. I tried to add to the blog but struggled to keep it positive. I feared that if I shared the reality, my phone would start to ring, and I didn't have the energy to listen to other people's fears about my husband's possible death.

I didn't want another Marna situation. Marna was a friend of Luke's from school. When she found out, she called screaming at me about how Luke taught her to change her oil and she couldn't face never learning anything else from him. I understood she was experiencing her grief, but why did Marna and others like her feel that sharing their pain with his caregiver was the right action? I think that may have been the point—they didn't think, they just felt their emotions and let them loose. Nope, no more of that. I decided to write at length about the amazing nurses on the floor and only briefly about Luke staying positive and doing well enough.

With each passing day, another new member of Luke's cancer team appeared, but our final day of chemo treatment was the worst. Someone from every division of the entire hospital showed up to provide advice. Chaplain, physician's assistants, doctors, and nurses—all wanted to be sure we knew what to do in any situation that could come up. They had good intentions, I'm sure, but it was overwhelming. It felt like even the café barista came by to make sure I knew how to brew Luke's coffee. The nutritionist gave me a gigantic three-ring binder filled with information and recipes. I love to cook, but it seemed strange to discuss feeding Luke when he felt his worst. Yet I needed to learn. No more Thai chili enchiladas: there was too much sugar in them for now.

We had to track where he was in treatment and make food according to that. When he left the hospital after five days of chemo, his blood cell count would continue to go down (what the doctors and nurses called *nadir*). We had to be careful with food then. As his body built his various blood counts back up, we could be a little looser with foods, especially on Chemo Eve, our name for the night before he signed up to get sick again. For now, avoiding sugar appeared to be one of the most significant directives.

Once Luke was on his last bag of chemo cocktail, he was suddenly full of energy. He began packing his things and lining them up near the doorway's wall. When the nurse gave us the green light to leave, we were on our way.

As we headed out the door, a photo seemed important to document a victorious end of the first round of chemo. Luke paused only for a second to shoot me an irritated look, signaling he was done and didn't need that memory. After snapping a handful of images in the hope that one would turn out, I grabbed my bag and ran to catch up with him.

WHEN WE GOT HOME, instead of rushing into the house at the same speed he left the hospital, he stood frozen. I grabbed a few bags from the back of the car and headed toward the front door. When I turned around, Luke was out on the curb, looking at our home with a faraway expression.

As I approached, his tears glistened in the sunshine. I put my arms around Luke and lowered my head to his shoulder. He tipped his head on top of mine. "I thought I'd never see this house again," he said with a catch in his voice. We stood there, holding one another together for a few moments. We stayed there until he began to move, then we quietly unloaded the rest of the car.

Halfway up the path, Luke stopped and looked around the yard. "Someone mowed our lawn and weeded our flower bed? That's amazing." I paused, noticing for the first time. We both looked up, and a few neighbors were waving from their windows across the street. We waved back.

Luke barely dropped his last bag in the house before rushing as best he could next door to pick up Westy. I watched through the window as our girl bounded around the yard, chasing Luke back to the house. His breath heavy from running a short distance, he dropped onto the couch and was immediately covered in Westy's kisses. Once the lovefest was over, she came to greet me briefly before sitting beside the couch where Luke was already sound asleep.

TWO DAYS WENT BY, and we pretended to be back in our ordinary life as much as possible. Luke slept most of the time but spent a few hours tinkering in his woodshop when he felt up to it. Meanwhile, upstairs in my home office, I was developing a branded series for a client about maintaining data security systems to avoid being hacked. Writing scripts that were similar to the work I'd been doing ten years ago made me feel a little raw. It was like someone had hacked into and reorganized my life. I had lost my talk show. Now was I backsliding? Should I even care? Should I have insisted on keeping my show? I angrily banged out the script, feeling guilty for the fury when I should have been grateful for the flexibility.

Luke went to bed around eight o'clock while I stayed up watching *Dateline*. Nothing like a good murder to distract me from my normal life. One woman had lost three husbands under suspicious conditions before finally getting caught putting cyanide in her fourth husband's morning coffee. I was fascinated by the story of how she managed to find these men and take advantage of them and their extensive insurance policies. Then a voice broke my concentration.

"You planning something, my dear?" Luke asked, peeking around the corner. "I don't think my life insurance policy is very high right now. Maybe you should increase the amount so you can be a wealthy widow." He laughed.

"Not funny," I growled, refusing to look up and reveal my true emotion.

But that was my Luke. Joking was his coping mechanism. When I met Luke, he had a dog named Belle. Belle was a fluffy German shepherd that he'd had since she was six weeks old. They had grown together through his twenties and through a marriage, divorce, and second marriage before she passed away at sixteen years old. I had been in the picture for six years by then, and my heart broke as we drove her to the vet to say goodbye. It was the first time Luke and

I had to deal with grief together. I cried all the way there, and Luke cracked jokes about all the things she could do in heaven that her old body had no longer allowed. This was his way.

I AWOKE AROUND TWO O'CLOCK IN THE MORNING, soaking wet. In a pool of sweat, sound asleep, Luke was gasping for air again. I grabbed a towel with cold water and wiped his face, which woke him up. Before he knew it, I had the thermometer sanitized and in his mouth. He had a temperature, but it wasn't high enough for him to go to the hospital. Flipping through the medicine cabinet, I only found Advil.

Keys in my trembling hand, I was throwing on my shoes when Luke got up. He quickly pulled on a shirt and a pair of jeans.

"I'm going to run to Safeway. You stay here," I ordered.

"No way, ma'am. You are not going to that sketchy grocery store in the middle of the night without me."

I fought him, begging for him to rest, promising I'd be right back, but he did not back down. I gave up. We left Westy to guard the house while we took a trip to the store.

Walking the short distance from the parking lot to the entrance of the twenty-four-hour Safeway, we saw a group of people shooting up in a corner; inside, more people looked vacant as they wandered the store. This unpredictable scene was why Luke didn't want me here alone. Everyone was wandering around, absorbed in their chaos, so no one paid any attention to me. Still, I wanted to move fast to get home soon. I kept turning around to make sure my slow-moving husband with the sweaty brow was able to keep up.

We arrived at the aisle with pain medications and found a large container of Tylenol. I headed back up to the register. Luke waved his hand to signal I needed to keep moving, saying he'd catch up with me in a moment.

I was amazed by how many people waited in line, even at this ungodly hour. We were third, behind a twenty-something woman who was carrying two filthy stuffed animals and buying four cases of soda and two bags of candy, and an elderly lady in a floral housedress whose cart—filled with lunch meat, bread, and cheese—was supervised by her Chihuahua. It was a sight to see. I added a bottle of cold water to our purchase at the last second. Before we left the store, I had Luke take the Tylenol.

That night, Luke slept soundly and seemed to cool down. I sat next to him, watching him sleep and feeling his forehead. If I slept and he got a fever, what would happen? Maybe tomorrow I could nap once I knew his fever was gone.

13

IT WAS HARD TO BELIEVE IT WAS ALREADY OCTOBER. The weeks had moved quickly between working, taking care of a sick Luke, and cooking foods that I hoped Luke would or could eat. I had lost track of time. But here we were, our last day at home before Luke started chemo round two. Finally, Luke was up and about and feeling much better. As the sun peeked out over the mountains and my night shift of watching Luke ended, I lay down and fell fast asleep.

When I woke a few hours later, I could hear Luke on the phone asking someone to come over. I dragged myself into the kitchen to get a hold of the miracle liquid called coffee. Luke came in and kissed me on the cheek.

"You may be a little mad, but I just asked Ronnie to come over. She has been texting me nonstop to see if you are ready to apologize yet."

I sighed. I knew I had to make this right, but I was not in the best mood. "When?"

"She'll be here in an hour."

I rushed into the bathroom to get cleaned up and ate a few hard-boiled eggs. Hopefully, the coffee and the eggs would fortify me against the storm that was about to blow into the house.

When it was just about time for Ronnie to appear, Luke decided to take Westy on a walk alone. I didn't even have to ask. I knew he was trying to give me space and avoid the drama to come.

Soon, Ronnie walked into my house and sat in the oversized wingback chair near the door, her lips tightly closed. I sat down on the footstool. I tried to look into her eyes, but she turned her head farther to the side.

"I'm sorry," I said, leaning in and touching her leg. "It's hard for me to admit what's happening, and I wasn't sure how to tell you. I wasn't sure what to say. I'm still not. I don't even know how I'm feeling."

She turned her head and looked straight at me, lips still pursed. Her tense face was so familiar. This was the expression she'd had when I borrowed her favorite soft-pink cashmere sweater, refused to leave the TV room when she had friends over, or hid her coveted do-not-ever-touch-these white chocolate macadamia nut cookies. This expression had successfully tortured me my whole life. The only way to counter this anger was touch. If I could get her to embrace me, I knew she would be on her way to forgiveness. The added eye contact made me brave.

"May I hug you?"

She nodded. I awkwardly reached for her over the chair. She hugged me back and sniffled. I leaned back to find her crying.

"I'm the big sister. I take care of you," she said, wiping mascara all down her cheeks. "Can you see how this made me feel?"

"I'm so sorry, Ronnie."

Ronnie leaned forward and kissed my forehead. "So, tell me, what is going on?"

I explained Luke's treatment plan, and she sat back and listened to every word. I kept touching her hand, trying to make up for my fear of telling her.

"I just don't know what to do, other than stuffing my feelings and holding on. And that is my plan. I just need to smile, make the best of it, and sort it out with a therapist when we get to the other side. And when I try to talk to Luke . . ."

Ronnie laughed, shaking her head. She grabbed my shoulder. "So, where is the cancer boy?"

I cringed. It was incredible how fast she could go back to being a turd. I didn't know whether to laugh at her predictability or cry. "On a walk with Westy."

"Well then, I should wait for him to get back before I share my big news!" Ronnie said.

I still felt sorry for hurting her feelings, but I was too tired to listen to a dramatic story. I started to tidy up the room. I moved magazines from the top shelf to the bottom and put the coasters back in a stack. "What are you doing for dinner? Luke and I will get a good meal before tomorrow's check-in at the hospital. Want to join us?"

"Where are you going?" She paused dramatically. "If it's good, then maybe I'll consider a family dinner."

"Luke wants chicken and waffles from Frank's Oyster House."

"You paying?"

I felt I had to, so I nodded.

"I'm in!"

Luke walked in the door five minutes later, happy to see Ronnie and me gabbing about her newest project redesigning a kitchen for an east-side couple. She had been without a single assignment for a while, a common theme for her freelance work life, so this was great news.

Luke sat down to listen for a moment, and Ronnie basked in the attention. She blathered on about which kind of marble she would put in their kitchen and explained the import process.

"But now that Lukie is here, I can tell you both my big news."

"Let's pause that. It's about dinnertime. Can we get in the car and head to Frank's? Ronnie is going to join us." Luke shot me a look. I ignored him, got up, and grabbed the keys. I could tell he was mildly irritated but still willing to go along with the plan.

TO LUKE, driving was joy and freedom. The freedom he was about to lose for five days while poison was pumped into his body to kill the likes of Arnie. Even the short trip to Frank's Oyster House, Luke relished. He dropped Ronnie and me off before searching for a spot on the charming tree-lined side street.

Inside, Ronnie and I took opposite sides in the large booth assigned to us. She rambled on about the kitchen, her hands fidgeting with the napkin. I leaned back and listened to the redundant story. My head began to bob forward.

"You're not falling asleep on me, are you? Remember, you aren't out of the doghouse yet!"

After another few minutes of Ronnie blathering on about herringbone tile, we ordered our drinks: a cosmopolitan for Ronnie, a nice crisp Chardonnay for me, and a rye old-fashioned for Luke. I wasn't sure that was what he'd want, but this was usually his first choice.

Luke slid in next to me at the table just as the server dropped off the drinks.

"Cheers to family, health, and hot men," Ronnie said, winking at Luke.

He kissed me on the cheek before we all clinked glasses.

"To Chemo Eve, a time to enjoy good food before the lockdown. It's kinda like the Last Supper I get to have six times. Lucky me!" Luke said, raising his glass again.

"Are you ready?" Ronnie asked as she tapped her spoon on the table.

Luke and I looked up. "Okay, shoot, Ronnie," Luke said before returning to the menu.

"Maybe you don't know this, Lukie, but my ex-boyfriend, who I broke up with, was declared Sexiest Man Alive by *People Magazine*. Of course, this reminded me of him in so many fond ways." She stopped for effect. "Seeing his face, I remembered how much he adored me and I felt I should give him another chance."

I caught myself copying her movement, gulping my wine.

"Did he call?" Luke asked.

Ronnie fussed with the edge of the tablecloth. "Well, not exactly." She threw her hands in the air. "But he did answer my call. And he sounded incredibly excited to hear from me." She leaned forward. "We talked for about thirty minutes. He didn't ask to get back together, per se—poor guy was probably scared to risk another rejection! But it was clear that he wants me back. So I put the man out of his misery and invited him to visit." She smiled and waved her hand in the air, signaling for another cocktail.

"And he said?" I asked.

"He jumped at the chance, asking for a few days to sort out the details. You know, he's a busy guy and can't just jump on a plane from LA to Seattle at a moment's notice."

I looked over at Luke, who was swishing his drink in circles.

The waitress's arrival prevented us from mentioning our obvious concerns about this story. Instead, we ordered a dozen oysters, two steaks, and Luke's beloved chicken and waffles.

"Don't worry. I will keep you both posted," Ronnie promised. She slurped her drink. Some drizzled down her chin and she wiped it up with the back of her hand. "I guess I'm going to have to get some new sexy clothes. It wouldn't be surprising if the paparazzi follow him and end up camping outside my house for a few days. But enough about me. Lukie, how are you feeling?"

"I'm feeling damned good. I have some crispy chicken and waffles coming!" Luke said as he took a swig of his old-fashioned.

The oysters arrived with two fresh mignonettes. Each of us enjoyed our share of the salty delight. Our main dishes arrived, and we ordered another round of drinks. Luke dove immediately into his fried chicken and grinned at the grease shining on his lips and chin. This look of pleasure made me smile. I put my hand on his knee and kissed his cheek. He squeezed my leg.

"Enough, you guys. You're so gross. What the hell are you guys actually doing at the hospital, anyway?"

"Chemo," Luke answered before taking another bite of fried chicken.

Ronnie rolled her eyes. "Duh. I know you have cancer and stuff, but, like, what do you do while you're stuck up there for five days?"

"Oh, good god, Ronnie. Do you have any manners?" I gave her a stare, warning her to knock it off.

"That's not gonna work on me today. Watch it, missy. You are barely forgiven. Remember that when you bitch at me."

Luke jumped in to avoid a confrontation. "They connect me to a chemo holder, and I walk, watch TV, sleep, and do whatever I can up there for five days while they pump poison into my veins."

"That sounds terrible. All those sick-looking bald people gross me out. I mean, I'll keep visiting, but just know I HAAAATE it," Ronnie said.

While this sounded rude, I hoped it meant that her visits would be minimal. Luke nodded and switched the topic of conversation. Now that Ronnie was drunk, she was easy to get going in any direction we wanted. He picked movies. I kissed him again, a sign of approval.

14

WHILE LUKE CHECKED IN, I got in the long line at the hospital Starbucks with all the doctors and patients waiting for their caffeine. By the time the coffee was ready, Luke was gone. I grabbed my bag and headed up to the oncology floor.

As the elevator doors opened, Lara's head popped up over the desk, where she sat talking on the phone. She pointed to a nearby room. Inside, *The Price Is Right* was on and Luke was spinning the wheels of the chemo caddy stationed in the room.

"These wheels are too tight. See how they don't spin freely? This is going to be a slow track week unless I do something about Richard."

We peeked out into the hallway, tempted to check the other rooms for a faster caddy, just as our older friend swept by with her sweet smile and a green floral embroidered jacket with matching hat and purse. We smiled back. She waved and continued her journey.

"See, she's moving fast. Her caddy has a different setup. Let's follow her!" said Luke.

"You are NOT going to steal that nice lady's caddy!"

"If I did that, I'd have her chemo, and that would be no good for anyone." He laughed, following our friend. I tagged along, unsure what he was doing.

"Aha!" he said as he caught up.

The lady turned around and tipped her head, knitting her brows inquisitively.

"I just wanted to look at your wheels." He pointed. She shook her head, still confused. He knelt and showed her the wheel. She smiled and nodded. It seemed more like she agreed that he was strange, not that she understood what he was saying. He smiled back, and she resumed her walk.

As she walked away, Lara appeared behind us. "Your chemo is ready, my friend. Shall we?"

THE FOLLOWING DAY, Luke's skin looked dull and his eyes glassy when he woke up. His favorite nurses weren't here today, he'd discovered earlier. A new nurse he didn't like had come in to change out the bag of chemo while I'd been sleeping, he told me. Just after he dozed off again, a woman in her sixties shuffled into the room. She wore animal-print scrubs and a frown. The nurse began the usual routine of checks, but she was gruff. We so loved the friendly banter with the other nurses that this curt approach left me uneasy.

As she set Luke up with another bag of chemo, he awoke and looked startled.

"This has to happen now," she said. Luke stared at her. "You understand?"

Luke settled back into his pillows without a word. I left the room to get us fresh coffees, hoping this might cheer him up. Unfortunately, the Starbucks in the lobby had a line of at least fifteen people. So even though I wasn't in a hurry, I walked to the other Starbucks about four blocks away through the series of glass tubes that connected many buildings and allowed pedestrians to avoid busy streets and the rain.

I bought a soy latte for me and a venti drip coffee for Luke. As I left the store with the drinks in hand, someone grabbed my arm.

"Please, ma'am, I'm cold and thirsty. Can I please have a coffee?"

I looked into the eyes of a woman with dull, weathered skin and a weak smile.

"What's your name?"

"It's Queenie, ma'am."

"Queenie, what would you like?"

She explained her rather complicated order, which included half-and-half milk and hazelnut syrup.

"Bless you, my dear girl," Queenie said when I returned with her coffee and a bagel. Standing there, staring at her as she went back outside and sat on a bench at the bus station, I couldn't help but think, *What if that were me or Luke? What if that woman had cancer and couldn't get treatment?* I felt paralyzed with fear. I brushed against a man in a suit who pushed me off him into the wall, spilling my hot latte all over my clothing.

"This is the line, lady. Don't stand here."

My moment of gratitude for my situation faded. In its place was anger. "You've got to be kidding me, man. Do you plan on replacing my coffee?"

He turned his back on me and made a call.

One barista had seen what happened and yelled that they would replace my order. I plunked into a chair, sure that my fury showed not only on my red face but in the steam that must've been billowing out of my ears.

Once my coffee was ready, I got out of there. Mr. Spiller Guy sat inside, eating a muffin, drinking his coffee, and continuing some jovial conversation on his phone. Jerk!

I rushed through the indoor tunnel like a mouse trying to find its cheese. In five minutes, I was back in Luke's room, offering him coffee and the story of why I had been gone so long.

AROUND TWO O'CLOCK IN THE AFTERNOON, I got sluggish. I craved another hit of caffeine, so I headed down to the lobby Starbucks for a cheap refill of black coffee to perk me up.

The line was long again but moving fast, so I decided to stay the course this time in my coffee-spotted shirt. Putting my used paper cup on the counter, I asked for a refill. The three employees behind the counter shook their heads and glared at me. I stared back, waiting to see what the problem was.

"Ma'am, this is not a holiday cup. It's a normal cup. We only have holiday cups right now. So are you trying to cheat the system and get cheap coffee?"

People in line behind me began to grumble. I shook my head and explained that I had gotten that cup from the other Starbucks earlier this morning. This barista insisted I was incorrect, that no one had these cups. The difference was only about a dollar, but I was still angry, and now I was embarrassed. I didn't want to give in.

We stood there staring at one another until the guy behind me said, "Lady, if you don't have the money, I'll pay for it. Just get out of the way. Some people have places to go."

"Fine, I'll pay for a drip coffee."

The barista left to pour the coffee, and I stood to the side, waiting and trembling with fury as I tried to ignore the glares from people in line. As she put my coffee down on the counter, our hands touched. She pulled hers away as if I were diseased.

"My husband is upstairs on chemo, possibly dying, and you want to fight me about a refill? Are you kidding me? Check the Starbucks on Madison to see if they started the Christmas cups yet." I turned away, but tears ran down my face. Finally, I had the attention of all the baristas. "Realize that you have a lot of power here and you just helped break me. Give me your names. I'm calling corporate when I get upstairs."

The room seemed to stop and stare at me. But instead of annoying glares, now their faces were filled with pity. No one spoke.

"I'm not kidding. Give me your names. Now."

They apologized and told me their names. I stormed out of the café, slamming my feet to release the electric fury pulsing through my body. By the time I got up to our room, I was sobbing.

After hearing my story, Luke asked me to cuddle up with him. I curled in and closed my eyes, wishing we were home on our bed, listening to the light snores of Westy as she slept.

"YOU KNOW, I love it when the coffee kicks in and I realize that I'll be able to whoop ass today. Caffeine runs in my blooooooood."

"Me too. Coffee is the most important meal of the day."

I opened my eyes to see Becca sitting in a chair in the room, laughing with Luke.

"You didn't tell me how funny Becca is! It's about time she and I met!" Luke smiled as I sat up.

It turned out their jokes about coffee were spurred on by my behavior—Becca had been downstairs in line and witnessed my explosion at Starbucks firsthand. My face reddened.

"I'm so embarrassed. Ugh, I can't ever go downstairs again!"

"It's normal. People in that line are often stressed. But in my opinion, they got what they had coming," Becca assured me.

"I could have been more graceful. Or spoken to the baristas more quietly and not made a fool of myself. Even the stuffed animals in the gift shop looked sorry for me." I looked down to avoid eye contact. "How's your mom?"

Becca shrugged. "They've enrolled her in yet another new trial. So, I guess there's hope, but we've been here so many times. They tell us there's a promising trial. We sign up, praying this is the cure. Within a few weeks or a few months, we end up with the same story: her cancer continues to spread, and the trial isn't working. That's when I see my mom lose hope, and I get angry."

"I'm sorry," Luke said. I reached over and squeezed his shoulder.

"I have yelled at the doctors more than once. I'm not proud of it. But it's happened. The thing is, the nurses assured me this is normal. This is life and death. They told me to give myself a break. Now I'm telling you the same." She smiled. "Anger is an underappreciated emotion, but it can be useful. It releases the tension in your body and acts as a strong motivator to take action. Use it to your benefit." Becca stood. "I need to go, but see what kind of gift the anger can bring."

I felt frozen. I barely managed to mutter a goodbye as my brain swam. Useful? I had never thought of anger as useful—something that could help me make the world better instead of attacking some poor kids working at a Starbucks.

"You okay?" Luke asked, rubbing my back. "You have that far-away look again. What's going on in that noggin?" He ran his hand down my long hair.

"I'm old enough to be her mother, yet she's teaching me."

I WAS DRIFTING OFF while reading a *People Magazine* article about another breakup in the Kardashian family when something caught my attention—jangly bracelets clinking back and forth. Opening my eyes, I saw Ronnie's shaking wrist in my face. This was a routine that Ronnie did often growing up. As a teen, I would fall asleep watching TV all the time. Ronnie would quietly walk in and stick her wrist in my face. She'd begin pumping her arm up and down so the bangles on her wrists would jangle. She'd do this until I opened my eyes. If I tried to ignore her, it would worsen with either a cup of water soaking my face or light slapping on my cheeks. I'd hated all of it, but opening my eyes to the jingles so she could laugh at how annoyed I looked had been the least offensive answer for me.

I smacked her hand away. "Fuck off, Ronnie. Just fuck off." My cheeks flushed as Ronnie pulled her hand back, brow knit with confusion.

"You relax!" Ronnie yelled.

Luke rolled over in bed. "Ladies . . ."

As he spoke, Ronnie's phone dinged. She picked it up and tapped in her code. Her face turned red as she digested the text. The color flowed from her cheeks down onto her chest. "Goddamn him." Ronnie's eyes filled with tears and a low grumble escaped her mouth. She sat down on the arm of my chair. Seeing how upset she was reminded me of the young woman deciding to unplug her parents. The memory erased the fury I had felt and replaced it with concern.

Ronnie put her phone in my lap and stood to pace the room. I looked down at the news article with a photo of Devan running on a beach with a young, stylish raven-haired woman.

"Who is that?" I asked.

"Damned if I know! I just talked to him last night, and I thought he was coming up to visit me and work things out. Just because I'm in my forties like him does not mean I'm not sexy!" Again Ronnie fidgeted, playing with the bracelets on her arms, this time not to annoy me but out of nervous energy and confusion.

"I'm sorry, Ronnie," I said, putting my hand on her shoulder.

"For hitting me, or because I look like a fool?" She glared, a vein popping out on her forehead near her hairline. I stood and tried to hug her. She pushed me away. "Give me my phone. I've got to get out of here."

I had barely lifted it into the air before she grabbed it and began furiously texting Devan.

I stared after her as she stormed out. Luke continued to watch TV, evidently finding the game show (or whatever show was on) much more entertaining than the ups and downs of sisterhood.

LATER THAT NIGHT, one of our favorite nurses arrived with a duster and a mop.

"Any chance you two are interested in taking one of your strolls?" Lara asked with a strange grin.

"Why?" Luke asked, staring at the unusual gear she'd brought with her.

"Someone named Ronnie called and read me the riot act. She mentioned how dirty this room was and told me it was unacceptable. Has this been bothering you?"

Luke's eyes darted around the room before settling in on me. "Are you kidding me? Damn your sister. Seriously." He then turned to Lara. "I'm so sorry, the room is fine. Ronnie is a drama queen and needs to stop. Don't worry about it. I'll handle it." Before Lara had exited the room, Luke had my sister on the phone.

Luke rarely gets angry. But when he does, he gets furious. My stomach hurt. Ronnie was already upset, and Luke was on steroids. This could be bad. Really bad.

"Ronnie, I will not accept your calling and making the nurses who are keeping me alive feel . . . Ronnie? Hello?" Luke looked over at me. "She hung up."

THE NEXT DAY, the silent ride home was a continuation of the discomfort I'd felt all morning as Luke finished his last bag of chemo and we left the hospital. Why did he seem so angry with me? He'd been grumpy as I packed my bags—"Really? You couldn't have done that earlier?"—and he'd refused to smile as I took a photo to mark the occasion. I had put an oversized grin on my face, hoping he'd pick up the cue. "Do it or don't, but I'm walking out of here in fifteen seconds," he'd said. I only took the pictures so that years down the road, we'd remember how he overcame cancer. Good or bad, this was a time we needed to remember.

I glanced at him from the driver's seat, trying to make eye contact with him across the car. He stared straight forward with a clenched jaw.

The neighbors that watched Westy must have seen us come home because before we were out of the car, she came blazing across their yard and jumped with joy around Luke and me. He reached down to pet her, then continued to the door. I let him go, squatting near my girl, who soaked my face in kisses. She popped her paw up on my shoulder and pushed me over. I couldn't stop laughing as she stood over me, continuing the lickfest.

"Are you guys coming or not?" Luke yelled from the porch. Westy went running as I picked myself up off the ground.

15

THE SECOND NIGHT HOME FROM THE HOSPITAL, Luke was hungry for pizza. Usually, I would roll my eyes, wishing for something healthier, but it was terrific that he was asking for food of any kind. Chemo can make even the most delicious cake taste terrible. So I happily jumped online and ordered a salad and the Brooklyn Bridge pizza piled high with salami, pepperoncini, olives, green peppers, onions, and mozzarella. Just ordering it made my taste buds water.

While we waited, I joined him on the couch. I always loved to lay my head in his lap so he could pet my hair. I assumed the normal position and waited for his gentle caress, but he started fidgeting with his legs instead.

"Can you get up? That's not comfortable." He squirmed.

"Sorry, love. I've just missed you."

"Well, it's not about you all the time, is it?"

I was shocked. Luke was usually gentle, and this felt like a slap to the face. I could find no words. Was I being selfish?

"I'm sorry. I didn't mean to upset you. Do you need me to be doing more? Are there things you need help with that I'm not doing? Things you wish I would do for you? Or am I talking too much? Too little? Tell me what I can do. I just want to be a help."

"Stop. Just stop. I want quiet." He got up and moved to a chair on the other side of the room. He tuned into the news, sipping a large glass of water while we waited for our meal. Westy sat next to him but stared back at me, her eyes wide.

Silence. I could give him that. I sat up and joined him in watching the TV. But I couldn't hear a word of what was said. My world was spinning. I was trying so hard, but clearly I was failing. He was miserable, and it was my fault. Well, not all my fault, but I wasn't making it better. I had been talking too much. I needed to be quieter and more helpful. I vowed to myself that I would be Charlie Chaplin. Fun but silent.

Westy exploded into wild barks, jumping around at the window, breaking our concentration on the local news. I could see the pizza delivery guy walking up the steps. I called for Westy to sit and stay and began opening the door, but Westy rushed to my side. I grabbed her collar. The kid backed up as far as he could get from us while still being on the porch. I squeezed through the crack in the door and shut it behind me.

"She's actually very friendly." I smiled.

"Sure." He handed me the pizza and the bag with the salad, his hands shaking. "You're all set, thanks." He ran from the porch and jumped into his car, then sped away.

I opened the door to a wagging Westy. She reached up and sniffed all over the box.

"I'm sure that smells good, girl." I laughed.

"Seriously, Mags, you knew she would go wild. Why didn't you get out there right away? That kid looked terrified." Luke shot me a look. "If that guy did something that scared her, she could become defensive, and then we'd lose her, and it'd be all your fault. Think, Mags. You have to think sometimes." His focus went back to the TV.

The pizza was hot. I turned and walked to the kitchen without a peep. Who was this rude man? I put the dinner down and went into the washroom to stop myself from making things worse by showing unwelcome emotions.

Through the door, I could hear Luke's and Westy's footsteps as they went into the kitchen to get their dinners, along with the clink of plates and rip of paper towels. Usually, I would insist on using cloth napkins, but Luke seemed irritable, so I would let it go.

"Don't stay in there and pout for too long, Mags. Dinner will get cold."

After I pulled myself together, I dished up a slice of pizza and a good heap of salad. My stomach was so twisted and my heart so upset that I had lost my appetite. I ate a few bites, wrapped it all up, and placed it in the fridge for later. I thought I might throw up. But trying to talk about it now was not going to help.

We finished dinner in silence. We watched TV in silence. Finally, we cleaned up, brushed our teeth, and went to bed without a single word.

I lay down next to this man who seemed a stranger and wondered if this would be the first night we went to bed without kissing goodnight. He leaned over and kissed me. I gave a loud sigh of relief. Maybe tomorrow would be better. I would talk to Luke about his nasty outburst.

"Oh god, I knew you were mad," Luke said, darting up to a sitting position in bed. "You are so sensitive. I just want a little quiet, and you are so dramatic. I'm sick of this."

His face became red with fury, and he threw the pillow across the room. "Damn it to hell. Seriously, Maggie, I just want peace, and you are always chattering away and asking me how I feel. I'll tell you when and if I want to. You demand so much. I'm sick and fucking tired of your shit."

He stood and started pacing around our small bedroom. I watched, not knowing what to do. Soon he was walking so fast that he nearly tripped over a shoe. He kicked the offending footwear so hard it flew out of the room. "If I had somewhere else to go, I'd get the fuck out of here." He stormed out of the room, and I heard the couch creak. I stayed still. Westy licked my face, then curled up on the floor next to me.

Two minutes later, Luke was back. "You know what? You sleep on the couch. I'm the sick one. So I get the bed."

My eyes grew wide as I left the bedroom and lay down on the couch. Westy settled in next to me and licked my tears.

This angry Luke was someone I didn't know. This man was so mean and high-strung—*my* partner was kind, always making sure I was okay. A few months ago, after we moved into our dream house, Luke planned a surprise for me. While I was at work, he arranged for the burgundy walls we detested to be painted over in a yellow cream. As I entered the house and saw the new color—the brightness he'd added to these previously dark rooms—I jumped for joy. Luke stood proudly in the middle of the room, grinning from ear to ear.

That night, I had woken with a splitting headache. Luke noticed me getting up and asked what was wrong. When I told him, he immediately went to the spare room upstairs, blew up a mattress, and opened all the windows. He helped me get upstairs because I was unsteady, then he slept on the floor next to me to make sure I was okay.

Now we couldn't be sleeping further apart.

AN HOUR LATER, Luke was standing over me. "Good god, woman, now you're snoring so loud I can't sleep. I'm tired, and you are killing me. What the hell is wrong with you? Go upstairs or something. I just want to sleep." He ripped the blanket off me. "Go now. I can't take it anymore."

I looked into Luke's eyes, usually filled with love, and all I saw was fury. As soon as he went back to bed, I grabbed the twenty-four-hour oncology phone number off the refrigerator. Locking Westy and me in the bathroom, I tried to dial the number and dropped the phone. I picked it up again and started over, hitting the wrong numbers. Westy licked my face, bringing me back to the cold bathroom floor. I took a deep breath and dialed again. Success. I told the receptionist what was going on, and she assured me that a doctor would call me back within ten minutes.

Those ten minutes felt like ten years. I had the phone set to vibrate so the ring wouldn't wake the beast sleeping in the bedroom on the other side of the house. I answered it as fast as I could.

"Are you safe? Is he violent?" the doctor asked after I explained the situation.

"Yes, I'm locked in the bathroom. I'm so confused. My husband is not a violent person, not ever. I have never seen this side of him."

"Sometimes, the steroids that go with these chemo treatments can bring the anger out in the patient. This is temporary. If you don't feel safe, stay with a friend or family."

"How? What if he needs something?" I asked. "I can't leave him!"

"You have to weigh the pros and cons. Just remember, Luke is under the influence of a powerful drug. It's not common, but it does happen where the steroids make a kind person violent, and they hurt someone they love."

"He'd never forgive himself if he hurt Westy or me. How long could this last?"

"Sometimes hours, sometimes a few days. It's different with every person."

We wrapped up the call, and I lay on the floor, holding Westy, not sure what to do.

16

THE SMELL OF BREWING COFFEE wafted through the air. I rolled over on the inflatable bed I'd set up after the doctor's call, and there Luke stood with two clear glass mugs of black coffee. He sat down on the edge of the bed, and Westy rolled over to cuddle her enormous head into his lap.

Luke laughed. "So I see someone got an extravagant treat last night." He nuzzled her face while she licked his cheeks. "I'm sorry, Maggie. I'm not sure what got into me. I know I was a complete asshole, but I don't remember a lot of the night. Why are you up here?"

I looked into his eyes. The fury was gone. In its place was the twinkle I hoped to see.

"You scared us," I whispered, looking down. "I have never seen you like that."

He rubbed my back. "I'm sorry. I don't know what else to say. I just remember feeling amped up. Like my whole body was buzzing."

"I called the oncology line because I was scared. They told me that this was the steroids in your system, but their effects would pass. They even warned that you might get violent." I paused to take a sip of coffee and see how he was reacting. "And based on the look in your eyes, I agreed. So I don't know that we need to go over the details. But if you get that angry again, I may take Westy and stay overnight at my sister's."

"You thought I might hurt you? Why?"

"You were throwing things and yelling." His head fell to his chest. He stared at the gray carpeting. "Love, it wasn't you. It was the drugs. Let's focus on the bright side. You are back to being our Luke." I sat up next to him and kissed him all over his face.

"I love you. Thank you for keeping us all safe. I don't feel like myself. Sometimes I do, but most of the time I feel like the person I know myself to be is gone. And now I'm this weak, useless man. I'm clinging to you, which makes me feel terrible."

Luke shook his head and fell back onto the bed. Westy took this as a cue to lick his face. He chuckled.

"I get lost because I never know what to do. I know you are fiercely independent. So how do I help?" I asked.

"I don't know." Luke stared at the ceiling. "I really do not know."

"I think we are both lost. I mean, that Arnie, he's a total bastard!" I lay down next to Luke. "But thanks for telling me how you feel."

DAYS PASSED WITH NO INCIDENTS of steroid-driven rage. It almost felt like everyday life. Luke tinkered in his shop, and I caught up on my guilty pleasure, true crime TV. I was deep into an episode of *Deadly Women* the day before we were scheduled to return to the hospital when Luke came up from his shop and joined me on the couch. I lay down in his lap and we quietly watched the final ten minutes of the show. It turned out that, after a particularly troubling fight, the wife had poisoned the husband with an everyday garden seed she ground up and put in his screwdriver cocktail.

"What sounds good for Chemo Eve, honey?" I asked as the credits rolled.

"Not a screwdriver!" Luke said with a smirk. "You know, you could probably get away with murder after all these shows you watch."

I sat up to kiss his cheek, then whispered in his ear, "I guess you better be careful." I kissed him again.

He paused and thought for a moment. "Didn't you say there was some new place that has good tacos?"

"Oh, yes. I went there with Veronica. The tacos were to die for."

Luke tipped his head and looked at me suspiciously. "You tried a new taco place without me? That's worse than murder. That's torture!"

"Hey, sir, don't pass that sass on to me. I already made a scene once in the hospital coffee shop. Do you need me to do it again? You know I will."

Luke held me close and kissed my hair. "That sounds great. I'll finish up by five. Let's go for a happy-hour dinner."

WE SADDLED UP TO THE BAR on our stools, just the two of us this time. Since we were early, Pablo y Pablo wasn't too busy. Luke ordered a mojito, and I got my glass of wine. When they arrived, we toasted to a successful third round of chemo.

Our tacos, ten in all, arrived on a giant white platter. We got two of each flavor: charred broccoli, spiced steak, chipotle chicken, pork belly banh mi, and pork carnitas. They were all delicious. I was blown away by the charred broccoli, and Luke loved the pork carnitas. I always like something new and different. Luke goes for the tried-and-tested usuals. He's typically a good sport about trying new things but always goes back to the classic dish when given a choice.

"I've been thinking . . ." I started.

"Does it hurt?"

"Ha, ha. Seriously, why don't we plan a trip to Denmark once you are all well? It will give us something to look forward to."

Luke grabbed another taco and took a bite. "How about Hawaii? We've been there. It's nice and familiar."

"Exactly, we've been there. So why not explore a new place? We would have so much fun!"

"I like Hawaii. I know where everything is. It's beautiful, and it's fun."

I shook my head. "Whatever. It'll be your trip." I ordered a flan to finish off the night.

"Don't you 'whatever' me. It'll be our trip. I'll think about Denmark, okay?"

"Deal."

"Deal? Remember, we need to negotiate, not compromise, like Kim told us in counseling. So, what would you give me if I agree to Denmark?"

I sat there thinking for a moment. He was right. In our couples counseling, our therapist Kim explained that a compromise left one person lacking, so if we negotiate, everyone gets something and gives something up. With so much sacrifice in our world, I tried to think about what it could be.

Luke started to laugh. "Don't think too hard, your brain may fall out."

"Ha, ha. I was just thinking about Kim. But, you know whatever it is, it'll be good. You'll love it there, bike paths with fast-paced cyclists everywhere you look. Lots of public transportation and history."

"And sunshine?"

"Not necessarily."

"So, what will you give me if I agree to Denmark?"

"A trip to Denmark."

"Smart ass."

"A new experience."

"What if I like to know, for sure, that a trip will be good and sunny?"

"How do you know a trip will be good, regardless of where you go? It could be stormy anywhere. We could stumble upon crime, bad weather, mean people in any corner of the globe."

"Truth. Okay, let's do this. We will take both trips. But we'll decide which one first when this whole chemo/cancer fiasco is finally over. Does that sound fair?"

"Done." Walking out of the room, I knew I had accomplished something. He'd agreed to go international, even if it wasn't his first choice. Now we just had to make it through this special version of hell. But the way things were trending, I felt great.

17

THE NEXT MORNING, I stood in line at the hospital Starbucks, feeling like a regular now that two rounds of chemo were behind us. Moving closer, I recognized the barista with the purple streak in her hair, the one I'd yelled at over the coffee refill debacle. I had called the corporate office that day and reported the baristas on duty for their lack of sensitivity. I had been angry, but now I looked differently at the young woman, working to earn her way.

As I reached the front of the line, she looked up at me, and her eyes widened. "How may I help you?" she whispered.

I was silent for a moment, not sure if I should just order or acknowledge the elephant in the café. "I know I made a scene, and you may have gotten in trouble. I'm sorry about that."

"I was just trying to save the company money. I was up for a promotion and thought it showed leadership. It didn't." The young woman rolled her eyes.

I stared at her. Had she dared to roll her eyes at me?

She looked at my face and shook her head furiously. "Ma'am, I'm sorry. I didn't think about the situations of the people coming through my line. May I buy your coffee today as a small apology?" She grabbed a cup, her hands shaking.

I smiled. "Don't worry. I got it. And no, I'm not going to report you again." I paused, hoping the barista would calm down. "May I please have a soy latte and a venti drip coffee, under the name *Maggie*?"

For once, no one was in line behind me. So I stayed behind the register as she filled Luke's cup. "Is your job okay?"

"Yes, we were sent in for further sensitivity training."

"How long have you been with Starbucks?"

"About a year and a few months. I started at another store and moved here about a month ago. I wanted to work here because I'm going to nursing school. I like to see the medical staff. I find it inspiring."

"That's smart," I noted. The barista handed me my coffee. "Thank you."

"My pleasure," she said with a smile. "I hope your husband is healing well."

LARA POINTED TO A SMALL ROOM next door to the tiny room we'd stayed in last time. I peeked inside and saw Luke looking out the window. Our luggage on the floor near him was still packed.

Instead of heading directly into the room, I turned the other way and walked toward the larger ones. In one, I saw Becca asleep on the second bed near her mother, who was staring out the window. Two rooms away, the space was empty.

Still carrying my coffee, I returned to Lara at the front desk.

"What would I have to do to get us that larger room over there?" I smiled big, hoping to win her over. "Last time we had that tiny room, and boy, it's hard on my back."

"You planning to sleep at the hospital, Maggie?"

"I sure am." My grin grew. "I can bring donuts!"

Lara laughed. "Okay, I'll move you, but just this once."

I ran into Luke's room in time to stop him from unloading. "Good news! Don't unpack. We're moving up in the world."

"What have you done?" Luke asked.

"One word—donuts!"

Lara came into our room and grabbed a bag, looking pleased. "You have been upgraded. Let me show you to your room."

OUR NEW ROOM not only had a great view of Capitol Hill, but we could also see glimpses of Lake Washington and the city of Bellevue peeking out in front of the mountain range.

"A new view, a new experience."

"But the same ol' chemo." Luke smirked.

"Yeah, yeah, but this is a win," I said, jumping up onto my bed. "I even have my own TV!"

"Oh yeah? Maybe I can get the Nintendo to route to both! Let me figure this out." He jumped into action, trying to finish the setup before he got plugged into his chemo and Richard the caddy bogged him down.

I looked over and saw that this room had one of the caddies with the purple wheels, usually a sign of the newer chemo holders. "Is that one of the fast ones?"

"Yep!" Luke grinned ear to ear.

AS LUKE WAITED FOR HIS CHEMO TO ARRIVE, I headed down to the Top Pot Doughnuts to get a dozen. I had to keep my promise, didn't I?

Outside the door stood Queenie, the homeless woman I had bought a bagel and latte for last week. She gazed down the street into the city. I stopped in front of her and waited for her to look at me. When she did, I smiled. "Hello again."

"Hello?"

"We met a while back. I'm heading into Top Pot Doughnuts. Do you want anything?"

"Why?" she asked, her tone defensive. "What do you need from me?"

Instead of answering right away, I thought about it for a bit. "Do you know other people up here who may need some help?"

"Yes, yes, I do."

"If I bought a dozen donuts and some coffee, could you share?"

She paused. "I suppose so. Ensure there's an apple fritter in there and an old-fashioned for my friend Bob around the corner, and it's a deal. Any chance I can get a half-and-half latte with hazelnut syrup?"

"Deal." I smiled and went into the store to buy two dozen donuts and a single old-fashioned with no glaze for Luke. His favorite.

When I got back outside, a man sat next to Queenie.

"This is my friend Bob." Bob nodded. "Thank you," she said as I handed her the treats.

"My pleasure," I said, repeating the barista's words from this morning. I smiled, wondering if that exchange was more for me than for them as I walked away. I felt amazing.

I DROPPED THE DONUTS OFF WITH LARA, and she laughed. "I was just kidding."

"But we'll take them!" the nurse behind her yelled. "Thank you!"

"My pleasure!"

Luke was lying on top of his sheets playing Super Mario Bros. in his usual button-up shirt and shorts. He and Richard had not become attached quite yet. So I set his old-fashioned down on the tray and settled on my bed. He smiled, taking a bite out of the donut.

A new young nurse entered the room. "Hello, Luke. I'm Emma," she said, pulling the computer up to her and busily typing. She asked him the usual intake questions, which always started with "Why are you here today?"

"I wasn't feeling well a while ago, so they told me I needed to come back here for some kind of treatment," Luke said with a straight face. "So here I am."

"You're here to take chemo for your cancer, correct?"

Luke sat up. "What? I have cancer?!" he nearly shouted.

Her face went white and her jaw dropped. She slowly turned to look at Luke, seeming horrified by the possibility that she had just revealed his cancer diagnosis to him for the first time. He stared at her blankly. She turned back to the screen, looking sick.

Luke cracked his cute goofy smile. "Sorry . . . just kidding. I know I have cancer."

"Wow! You got me." She turned to me. "Is he always like this?"

I laughed. "Yup. Mr. Funny Pants is here for the next five days. You're welcome!"

THERE WAS ALWAYS an antiseptic, bleachy smell in the hospital. Sometimes it was more potent than at others. That night, the smells and the heat combined had Luke sweating his way through the sheets. I helped him into the bathroom, dragging along Richard the chemo caddy, his constant companion. As Luke got into the shower,

I struggled to set up Richard just outside it so that Luke could have some privacy from his chemo, at least for a moment.

"What is taking so long?"

"Richard's wheels are dead set on rolling into the curtain. I'm trying to get him all wedged into the corner." I pushed harder and harder. Finally, taking the door wedge from outside the room, I jammed it under one of his five wheels.

Once I heard Luke turn the water on, I went out to the nurses' desk, hoping for a quick sheet change. Luckily, someone could come into our room and make the swap before Luke got out of the shower.

"Am I safe?" he called from inside the echoing bathroom.

"Yes, sir."

He came into the room, naked other than his flip-flops, dragging Richard behind him. "Mind helping me with the antibacterial wipes?"

Popping to my feet, I grabbed the thick, plastic packets on the counter and opened the pads up. Luke raised his hands in the air, and I wiped the sticky pads all over his body. One for his arms, one for his torso, one for his legs, and one for his private area.

"After a shower, at least I get to feel clean for a few minutes," he joked. "That stuff feels like a coat of plastic being layered all over my skin."

I chuckled, then noticed he was swaying all over. I stopped for a second.

"Come on, let's get this done," he said, lifting his foot and wiggling it in front of me so I'd wipe the bottom. He wobbled again. I rushed to finish so he could sit on the bed.

His face looked paler, and I could hear his breathing. "Honey, you sound bad." He nodded, lying down on the bed, dropping the flip-flops as he went. He was snoring loudly within a few minutes. We skipped the last two wipes in favor of sleep.

EVERY NIGHT, the nurses came in and out of the room, doing the standard tests. I felt lucky that I got to sleep while Luke had to engage with them every four hours. How hard it had to be to heal with people fussing over you so much. But then again, I knew the nurses weren't doing this for their entertainment. I was glad they made sure the chemo wasn't affecting him too strongly or damaging him in ways that didn't fight cancer.

This time, in between their visits, Luke was tossing and turning, struggling to breathe. I got up at three in the morning and sat on the edge of his bed, rubbing his back, wishing I could do more to help. Luke guided me to the left side of his back, asking me to feel a specific spot. The rattle coming from inside was so apparent it felt like a truck rumbling its way across a bridge. I propped pillows under his head and got him seated more upright, which seemed to help. He begged me to not get the nurses yet. I struggled with the idea of going against him but figured I could keep an eye on him and make sure it didn't get worse. The morning was only a few hours away.

A couple of hours later, I woke up before Luke. His breathing had a wheeze, and his color looked even more off than it had the night before. I crawled out of my bed and got dressed before heading to the nurses' station.

A few hours later, Doc Proc showed up with his cart containing the enormous needle to drain Luke's lung through his back. We woke Luke up, and he assumed the position.

"Don't worry, honey. You don't need to stay," Luke assured me. He knew I wasn't too fond of even a tiny needle. This gigantic needle was too much for me to bear.

I wandered toward the family room while they drained Luke's lung and found Becca curled up in a tiny ball on the couch, weeping so hard into her hands that her breath stuttered.

Sitting next to her, I slowly reached over and rubbed her back. She peeked through her hands, revealing her bloodshot brown eyes. "Sorry," she whispered between the sobs. I wished for the second time in only a few hours that I could do more, but merely sitting there quietly was all I could do. We sat this way for a few minutes before Becca grabbed tissues and blew her nose.

"Hospice just left," she said, starting to sob again. My stomach twisted into knots. Hospice meant that her mother's last trial was over. There were no more treatments. This young woman was alone, faced with losing her mother.

"They were kind. It's the right choice. I mean, I do not want to lose my mom, but she's in terrible pain. But what will I do without her? She is my best friend. My rock. My dad still refuses to come in. He doesn't believe she will die."

"I'm sorry, Becca." I continued to rub her back and dig through my brain for some way to help. What could possibly be helpful to my new friend? Then I had an idea. "Is there anyone you need to call?"

"My brother. I already called my dad. My brother is going to lose it, and I can't bear his pain and mine right now."

"I got this. Can you give me your brother's number?"

She handed me her phone.

"Hi, Justin. My name is Maggie. I'm at the hospital with your sister . . . Yes, your mom is still alive . . . No, your dad is . . . right . . . but I'm sorry to say that Becca just signed your mom up for hospice." The man on the other end of the phone broke down crying. My heart hurt for both of them. "Great. I'll let her know." I turned to Becca, who had calmed a bit. "He's going to grab the first flight and text you his information."

"What do I do, Maggie? What?" She leaned into my shoulder.

"You should be proud of yourself. You are choosing the right path for your mom. Helping your loved ones get out of pain is much harder than continuing to beg them to stay in treatment. Some time ago, Luke and I helped manage the end of life for an elderly neighbor. He had lived next door to my husband for over ten years when he was diagnosed with dementia. He didn't have any family, so we took care of him. One day, he broke his hip and went to the hospital. They operated and sent him into rehab. Every night at five o'clock sharp, he'd try to get out of his bed. He fell, pulling out his catheter. We met the ambulance at the emergency room. Between dementia and the pain, he was in bad shape. I had never seen such fear in someone's eyes. We talked and he was lucid enough to say, 'No more.' He began losing language and the ability to swallow over the next few days. We registered him for hospice care. We realized he wasn't going to get better and moving him to and from the ER was making his final days terrifying."

Becca nodded as I told my story. "How long before he died?"

"Only about a week." I felt sick to my stomach. "Sorry, this isn't about me. It's about you and your family."

"It's good to hear. The hospice nurses said they could treat her right here since my dad is so, so, so . . . difficult." She stopped and took a deep breath. "When I called him . . ." She paused, beginning to sob again. I grabbed her into a hug. She regained her composure. "My dad yelled that I was a liar. He said I wanted my mom dead. He said I was murdering her." She broke down again. I feared if I ever met this man, I'd punch him right in the face.

"Becca?" a nurse's voice whispered into the family room. "Your mom is asking for you."

Becca hugged me tighter. "Thank you," she said, taking a deep breath before turning on her heel.

"I'm here if you need me. Just come to our room anytime."

She nodded and disappeared down the sterile white hallway.

WHEN I FINALLY GOT BACK TO THE ROOM, it was quiet except for Luke's snoring. I didn't want to wake him. I carefully went to the chair next to his bed. Turning to sit down, I nearly screamed when I noticed Lara standing behind me in the doorway.

"Whoops! Sorry to scare you. I just wanted to let you know we didn't need to drain Luke's lung. His lungs are no longer filling with fluid."

"But that terrible rattle," I said. "What the hell is that?"

"It's likely that the pleura is reattaching to the lung. That could be creating that rattle. It will likely do that until Luke heals."

"Then why is he so listless and colorless?"

"Probably chemo," she said with a sympathetic smile.

18

CURLED UP IN MY HOSPITAL BED, I daydreamed of the ski vacation Luke and I had taken last winter. We flew to Sun Valley and stayed in a quaint little chalet. We'd lit the fire in the fireplace and sat on the floor drinking wine and listening to jazz music every night. Some nights we played cards; others, we just enjoyed one another. In my dream, I toasted him, and our glasses clanged. I went to sip the wine, but Luke hit my glass again and again until it broke and red wine was all over me. I sat straight up in my bed to find my sister sitting next to me, jangling her bracelets in my face.

"What the hell are you doing here this early?" I asked her as she lay down on my pillow, laughing hysterically.

"Gotcha!" she cheered, proud of herself.

I looked over at Luke sleeping. "What are you doing? It's only 8:00 a.m. I didn't realize you even knew the clock had numbers before ten," I whispered.

She laughed. "Like you're any better."

"Touché. You seem like you're in a good mood."

"He's coming. He's coming. He's coming! Devan finally saw the light and left that little twit in Geneva. He said he's flying directly back to me. I knew it. I knew he wanted me!" She wiggled with excitement and clapped her hands. "I can't wait to see him. But I need your help. What should we do? It's been a year or so since we broke up."

A loud yawn came from the other side of the room. "Good morning, ladies." Luke smiled. He looked so much better. There was a little pink to his cheeks. Luke's eyes locked in on Ronnie. "Hey, can you do me a big favor, Ronnie?"

"Of course, anything for you." She grinned. "What do you need? I can get you a discount on almost anything!"

"Can you get me a discount on sisters-in-law who don't yell at my nurses and embarrass me?"

"Oh, come on. I'm trying to keep you safe, not embarrass you. You don't need that dust."

"I'm not kidding. Do not treat my nurses like that." He stared at her. "Can you go apologize?"

"Uh, no. I was right, but if you insist, I'll keep my mouth zipped from now on and let your little cancer cells party with that dirt."

"Ronnie." His warning was in a deep tone he only used when he was on the verge of fury.

"Right, I'm sorry, Luke. I won't do it again. But hey . . . god, you look like death warmed over," Ronnie exclaimed, running over to hug him. I cringed at the statement, never knowing how close we were to that grim reaper.

"Thanks, you look great too."

Ronnie did a spin, throwing her long dark locks and short skirt into a twirl. "You really think so?"

"I think you should get a fancy hotel room and go sightseeing in downtown Seattle." I walked to Luke's bed and sat next to him, rubbing his arms. "How are you feeling, honey?"

"Like the Four Seasons? That's perfect! You still know someone there who can get me a discount? I want to impress him, but I'm not made of money. What was her name? Lachelle? She still here?"

"Nope. Lachelle moved back east and isn't with the hotel anymore. So you'll have to sort this one out on your own."

"Could you call her and just see if she has connections?" Ronnie asked, tipping her head to the side, aiming to look cute and friendly.

"Nope." Luke's empty glass in hand, I walked to the other side of the room, where a nurse had placed a pitcher of ice water earlier, covered with Saran Wrap. As I pulled the wrap off the old brown pitcher, I thought about how much Saran Wrap they must have down in the kitchen. I poured the water and brought it back to Luke.

"Come on, sissy. You know you want to help me find happiness! Just make that one call. I promise I'll be nice."

Luke and I both started to laugh uncontrollably.

"What? I can be nice." Ronnie wrinkled her brow.

We laughed harder.

"I'll TRY to be nice." Her lips pursed into a tight pout, and she shook her head. "You guys are not funny." We kept laughing, which just made her angrier. "Okay, fine. I met her a few times. I'll call her myself. Remember, I did her a solid. Give me her number?"

It was true. One night a few months before Lachelle left, Ronnie had joined me and a few friends for a night of cocktails at a funky little pub. We had worked together ten years earlier and wanted to catch up, but Ronnie had other plans. She lobbied hard for karaoke. She wanted to sing "Let's Get It On" and see if she could find herself a date. After a couple of hours eating and chatting, we relented and headed a few doors down to the boat-themed Baranof to let her have her fun.

Inside, Ronnie quickly signed herself up for karaoke, and we grabbed a dirty booth in the corner.

Lachelle went to the bar and soon came back with three tiny airplane bottles of wine with plastic cups. "Ladies, I think we have found the place that puts the *k* in *class*."

We'd poured our wines into the red cups, toasted the plastic, and listened to Ronnie as she sang off-key. She wasn't a good singer, but she wiggled her hips and showed her long legs, so plenty of men were clamoring to get her attention. She came back to us with four in tow.

"Ladies, meet my new best friends." She turned to them. "What are your names again?" The men introduced themselves and sat down in the empty spaces. A few minutes later, one of the men's other friends, Joe, joined us. He sat next to Lachelle, and they'd been together ever since.

Once she had the phone number, Ronnie said her goodbyes and disappeared down the hall. I was sure she was going to pour it on thick. I almost felt bad for Lachelle, but then again, Ronnie had kind of been her matchmaker.

I GOT UP EARLY on the last day of Luke's chemo to wrap up a few more blog posts for work before he finished the last bag of chemo.

Today marked our official halfway point. Luke had completed three treatments and had three to go.

Two hours and about four nurse visits went by before I finished my work.

Luke woke up. He looked at me groggily. "How much longer?"

"Looks like about half an hour." Luke shook his head and fell back down on his pillow. Where was the guy who always leaped out of bed on the last morning of chemo and had his bags packed first thing? This behavior was out of character. I walked over to him and felt his head. He was hot.

The nurse came in to take his temperature: 99 degrees. He slept while we got the discharge papers all ready. I was concerned about taking him home, but they assured me it was normal to run slightly hot.

The nurses and I helped Luke out of bed. He was able to stand but was weak. As they got him into a wheelchair, I quickly packed his bags and rushed down to bring the car around. By the time I got to the circular drive, he sat at the door waving slowly with a half grin. I knew he wanted to go home, but I was worried. I jumped out of the car and offered my hand to help him up. "You sure you're okay to go home, honey?"

"The doctors cleared me. I'm tired, but that's normal. It's Halloween. I gotta be home for the kids. I'll be fine. Stop fussing."

Luke got into the car and heard the radio deejay announce the next song, "Escape." He laughed. "You must be worried to let me listen to Metallica."

19

WE COULD SEE WESTY'S EARS perked up through the neighbors' window. She must have heard the car.

I ran over to open Luke's door. "Welcome home, sir," I said, grabbing his arm and trying to help him out of the car.

"I got this," he said, slowly lifting himself to a stand and taking a moment to catch his breath. He took a few steps and turned. "Look at me. I'm walking."

"Not funny, mister. You seem unusually weak."

"I'm ignoring that. Let's just get inside."

I helped him up the five steps to the doorway and got him inside. "Where do you want to go?"

"Bed."

THAT NIGHT WAS HALLOWEEN. Luke brightened, ready to pass out candy with a Dr. Seuss hat resting atop his head. I worried this would further exhaust him, but he was so happy. How could I deny him that joy? So I sat watching as he praised each kid's costume, especially the ones that were homemade.

Near the end of the evening, three kids showed up dressed as little grim reapers. The smallest one had these little scythes. Adorable and haunting all at the same time. Next up was a miniature robot made from a box and tin foil, the buttons colored on by markers and toddler hands. Luke laughed, enjoying the creativity while I reflected on the grim reaper. He could come and collect any of us at any age or time. My stomach cramped, and shivers ran up my spine. Luke turned to me with a knit brow, cocking his head to the side. I knew this meant he felt the shift in my energy. I smiled and shook my head.

Luke turned back to the door, where a group of teenagers was returning. It was nine o'clock already, so he dumped the rest of his bowl into their bags and turned out the light.

THE NEXT TWO DAYS WENT BY SLOWLY. Luke slept a lot. I made sure he had a full water bottle and a couple of meals a day. Everything tasted terrible to him except oatmeal.

I sat in the living room, working on my work projects, keeping one ear tuned in to ensure he didn't need anything.

A few days after getting home, he felt a lot better and wanted to try being up for the day. He stood beside the bed and stretched. Holding vigil next to the bed, Westy immediately ran between his legs with her tail wagging vigorously. She sniffed up and down his legs.

"Yup, girl. I'm sure I stink." He bent down and kissed the top of her head.

We headed into the bathtub shower with the bright tulip-covered curtain. I sat on the edge of the tub while Luke took a shower. He could stand easily now, but I stayed with him to make sure.

"Check this out," he said, pulling out a large clump of hair. "It may be time for a new haircut."

I looked down. The tub was full of Luke's brown hair. The back of his head was a patch of small polka dots, but the dots were made of hair and not skin.

"I think so. Want me to get the clippers?"

The electric clippers sat in the back of a drawer. A flip of the black switch and the clippers jumped to life, their loud buzzing declaring a new cut was coming to town. Westy barked at the loud machine. I turned it off and held it out for her to smell. She took an intense whiff, then licked the handle.

More hair came off on the towel and fell onto the floor as Luke dried himself. Unsure how he was feeling, I looked at his face. He stared at the clumps of hair and shook his head. "Well, if you're going to do it, don't do it halfway. Let's shave it off."

I did what he asked, save one clump right at the front, so he looked like a Kewpie doll. I started to chuckle as I finished the back.

"What are you up to?" He turned to stare at me. I gave him a huge toothy grin. He turned the other way to face the mirror.

"It's a good look for me, don'tcha think?"

I grabbed my cell phone. Holding it up, I took a picture of him with a towel around his waist and a curled clump of hair right in the middle of his forehead. Then we both broke down laughing.

"Okay, enough shenanigans, shave that thing off so I can rinse off again. I want to make sure I'm rid of all that pesky hair."

I took it off, relieved that he seemed a lot more like himself. As the shower started, Westy and I left the bathroom.

THE NEXT SIXTEEN DAYS PASSED without much excitement. Well, other than the new experience of a bald head on the pillow next to me each night. The first morning I woke to the bald head, I reached out and rubbed it. This soft head was one I wanted to keep.

The day before chemo started, we got up and sat at our front window, watching people walk by with their dogs. Then we curled up with our cups of coffee and sat in silence with Westy at our feet.

"We're halfway through treatment. I think tonight we should make reservations. Let's go to Daniel's, get popcorn shrimp, amazing steaks, and enjoy the night," Luke offered.

I smiled. "You got it."

I called Daniel's. They had no reservations available until nine that night. I could hear Luke humming while he watched the news. I didn't want to disappoint him, so I went against our usual rule of not using the cancer card and redialed.

"Daniel's, how may I help you?" the young woman asked.

"Hello," I said, sneaking upstairs to prevent Luke from hearing me. "I realize this is last minute, but my husband is going through chemotherapy. Tomorrow, he goes in for his fourth round of chemo, and he's been dreaming of your popcorn shrimp and amazing steak. Is there any way you can squeeze in a table for two? Please?"

"I'm so sorry to hear this. Where is your husband being treated?"

"Swedish Hospital on Capitol Hill," I said, curious as to why she asked.

"My girlfriend works there. Please hold for a moment. What's your husband's name?"

"Luke Byrne." For a few minutes, I listened to Christmas music and invitations to join the frequent diners' club. My stomach was in knots. I knew that Luke would be annoyed at me for using the C card, but it would be worth it, right? I paced as I waited.

"Everything okay, Mags?" Luke shouted from downstairs. "Sounds like you're pacing up a storm."

"I'm good. Don't worry. I'll be down in a moment."

"Ma'am?" Her voice came back on.

"Yes?"

"You're in luck. I guess you know Lara? She confirmed he is a patient, so I'm happy to find you a spot for six o'clock tonight. That's the only space I have. You must also finish by eight. Is that okay?"

"We'll take it. Thank you, thank you!"

She laughed. "Lara said you guys are sweet. I'll see you at six. Ask for Nora when you get here."

"We're in!" I shouted. "We got in!" I heard Luke cheer from downstairs.

WE HANDED OVER OUR CAR to the valet at six o'clock on the dot and entered the luxurious restaurant. The lights were dim, and outside we could see the boats twinkling on the lake.

Luke took a seat, and I went up to the desk. "I have reservations under the name *Byrne*." I smiled. "Is Nora here?"

"Yes. Let me take you to your seat, and I'll have Nora come to the table as soon as she can."

"Fantastic!"

The hostess guided us by the glass box displaying different cuts of meat and passed the steamy kitchen, where staff worked behind the half wall to cook delicious steaks and seafood. Finally, we got to the back of the restaurant, where she seated us right next to the window. This table was one of the best seats in the house.

"Wow! Thanks," Luke said. He looked over at me. "How did we get this sweet, sweet seat so last minute?"

"Luck, I guess." I leaned across the table and kissed him.

He tipped his head in disbelief. Then, before he could question me anymore, the sommelier arrived and took our order for a fancy bottle of wine that would go with the steaks. But first, we would start with cocktails—an old-fashioned for Luke and a negroni for me.

"To health, happiness, and a good steak," I said, raising my glass. Luke clinked my glass and took a sip.

"Mmmm, delicious! It's been so long since I could even consider having one of these."

Then a woman approached our table.

"Luke?" she asked, scanning his bald head and thin eyebrows. He looked at her quizzically. "It's nice to meet you. I'm Nora. I heard all about your treatment starting tomorrow and how you love the restaurant. I'm so glad we could get you in."

"Me too," he said, tossing me a sideways glance. "How did you know?"

"Oh, when your wife told me about your situation, I wanted to check it out. It just so happens that my girlfriend, Lara, works in Swedish, and she vouched for you. You would be amazed at the lies people tell trying to get in." She smiled. "I've got a complimentary popcorn shrimp on the way for you. Do you need anything else before your server comes back to check on you?"

"No, I think we're good," he said, his voice tightening just enough for me to notice. I looked down at the table as Nora walked away.

"Maggie, that is so embarrassing. Seriously, you used my cancer to get us a table? That's awful. I thought we were on the same page. I can't believe you did this."

"I'm sorry. I wanted to get us in, and it worked." I smiled weakly.

"I am not happy."

We sat in silence for a few moments until the popcorn shrimp arrived. Luke's eyes grew wide as he grabbed a golden-brown fried shrimp and dipped it in the spicy sauce.

"Okay, maybe I'm a little happy. Let's enjoy tonight. But we will talk about this later, Mags."

I stuffed a giant shrimp into my mouth and began to chew.

20

THE NEXT MORNING, we got ready and drove to the hospital in silence. I knew Luke was upset about my using his cancer to get us into Daniel's, but I had hoped he'd get over it quickly. He had been pretty quiet for the rest of the dinner, but we did have a surface-level conversation during dessert.

Today was different. It was like Luke had gotten up on the wrong side of the bed. His lips curled downward, and he refused to make eye contact. I pretended to be upbeat all morning, but from the sheer number of sighs he made, I knew he wasn't going to get over it right away.

While I waited for our check-in coffees at the hospital Starbucks, Luke went upstairs and got settled. The girl I had yelled at was behind the counter again.

"Hello. Want your usual?" she asked with a smile.

"Sure do. Thanks."

"You look sad today. Everything okay?"

"Nah, my husband is mad at me and won't even talk about it."

"Sorry." She wrinkled her nose.

"We'll work it out." I held out my phone to pay for our coffees, then went to stand with all the other sad souls waiting for their daily hit of caffeine.

The next stop was the oncology floor. Just outside the elevator, I paused at that steely ONCOLOGY sign. Today it looked shinier. I felt like it was sharpening itself to cut my heart open. I stared at it, wishing I could sink into the ground and stop the pain. I felt sadder than I had ever felt. My body was heavy. My eyes felt wet. I put my hand on the first *O*. Cold. I leaned forward and rested my face against it. Luke was in a room somewhere, angry at me.

"Hey, we just shined that." I heard Lara's voice behind me. I straightened up and tried to smile.

"How was your dinner last night?" she asked.

My hands started to tremble. "It was good. Thank you for confirming that Luke is a patient here. Your girlfriend was great. She gave us complimentary popcorn shrimp." I tried to sound upbeat. "Hey, can I ask you a favor?"

"Sure, what do you need?"

"Don't mention the dinner to Luke."

Lara's lips tightened.

"You already did? Okay. Where is he?"

"He's over here," she said, walking me toward the room. "I'm sorry if I caused a problem. I was excited for you two to get a good dinner."

"I know. Luke's just mad I used the cancer card to score the reservation. He's pretty private."

"Ah, right. Understood. Mum's the word from here on out."

"Thanks," I said, stepping into the room and running my hands below the machine so the foamy sanitizer could wash away any germs and, hopefully, my bad choices.

Inside, Luke had his room all organized just how he likes it. He was propped up on pillows, staring out the window, waiting for the chemo to start.

"So, you want to talk about it?" I asked.

"You know what you did," he said matter-of-factly.

"I'm sorry. I'm so sorry. I didn't mean to upset you." He nodded. "Plus, I wanted that shrimp and steak too." I smiled at him.

He looked away. "My cancer is not a tool to get your way. Why did you have to do that? We could have gone somewhere else."

"I suppose. You just seemed so excited. Please forgive me. I promise to not use the cancer card again." I held my right hand up and put my left on my heart. "Scout's honor."

"We could have just planned to go to Daniel's another day. Or we could have invited friends over. How about that?" He crossed his arms.

"What? That would be weird right now. We haven't talked to many of them in weeks. I keep asking them to go to the website instead of calling. Plus, most don't seem to know what to say to either one of us. Do you want to spend the evening explaining what's been going on?"

"Suppose not."

"Well then, can we let this go?"

He turned and looked at me for the first time since last night. His eyes shone with forgiveness but not acceptance. I could tell he was still working through the embarrassment.

"I'm going to let you have some space. Text me if you need me."

"Yup."

I FOUND BECCA CURLED UP in the family room, reading a book.

"What you reading?" I asked her. She jumped in surprise, then smiled. She held up *Where'd You Go, Bernadette*. "That's a fun one. Plus, it takes place here!"

"Yeah. I grew up on Queen Anne. I know the kind of mothers she is talking about because they drove my mom crazy. She didn't go with the flow. That always inspired me."

"How is your mom?" I asked, reaching out to touch her arm.

"Not good, but still here. My brother came up and visited for a few days, but he's gone again. He and my dad don't get along, so he wanted to get out of there. His excuse is that she's rarely awake." I shook my head. "My dad still hasn't come either. He is insisting I'm trying to murder her but she's on to me, so he thinks she'll be coming home." I slid over and hugged her. Seeing Becca cry made my eyes well up too.

"Your dad thinks you're trying to kill her? Does he see what you do? Do you want me to call him?" I wished I could do something to help this young woman I respected so much.

"Nah, that won't go very well. I'll try again tomorrow." Becca wiped her face. "Enough about me. How are you doing?"

"Eh, I don't know. I feel sadder than ever, ha. I got in trouble with Luke last night. He wasn't speaking to me. I'm in here giving him space because he's still mad."

"What happened?" she asked, her face brimming with compassion.

I looked away in shame. "I messed up." I put my hands over my face, and she rubbed my back as I filled her in.

When I finally caught my breath, I looked at Becca's face. She gave me a sympathetic smile.

"I've gotten in trouble for that too. When my mom was well, I did it to get us free tickets to *Hamilton*." She laughed. "We had a great time, but my mom was super pissed when she found out. But you know what? She realized that my heart was in the right place, so she forgave me. I'm sure Luke will too." She leaned in and whispered, "And I'd say at least in my case it was worth it."

I couldn't help but laugh. "Thanks, Becca."

ON MY WAY BACK TO LUKE'S ROOM, I saw the smiling lady. She had leaves and pink flowers embroidered on a seafoam-green top. Her pants fit loosely, and the purse was green with gold glitter. She walked with a smile, looking like she was on an afternoon stroll through the park. I admired her attitude. Who was here with her and how many outfits had she brought? I smiled and waved. She grinned. Just before I got to Luke's room, I saw Lara.

"Hey, what is the story with the smiling lady?" I asked.

"Ming? She has had cancer for years but continues to beat it. I think it's her attitude, to be honest." She smiled, watching Ming round the corner and go out of sight. "She's an amazing woman."

"She makes me smile."

"Me too!" Lara said before she walked into the room next to Luke's.

Luke was sitting up on the edge of his bed. "Just finished the steroids, and I feel anxious. Want to go for a walk?" He stood, grabbing Richard and heading out the door.

Usually, we avoided the other side of the oncology floor, which housed patients with different types of cancer than Luke's. That side always seemed darker.

Today, Luke didn't care. He needed to work out the energy. We did a figure-eight loop around the floor, peeking into rooms with ill people surrounded by family. The guests ate and chatted, acting as if all was normal, but each of them had an air of grief about them.

Just as we were about to return to our side of the floor, I saw an old colleague standing against the wall in the hallway. I stopped.

"Denise?"

She looked up and smiled. "Hey there. Remind me of your name? You worked at Humongous, right? Back in the nineties?"

"Yeah, I did. I'm Maggie."

"Right, right. What brings you here?"

"My husband has lymphoma, and he's an in-patient for five days. So here we are. You?"

She pointed at the door in front of her. "My friend Michael is a deejay I've worked with for years. He's rad. About six months ago, just before turning thirty, he found out he had cancer. Now I have to say goodbye. The treatments aren't working."

The door across the hallway opened. An older man with gray hair and a tear-stained face looked out. "Denise, want to come in?"

Tipping my head, I stole a peek into the room. Inside, a young bald man looked gray and bony. His head was turned toward the door, but his gaze seemed vacant. I wondered if he was gone already. Then, just as I began to worry, I saw him blink.

I put my hand on Denise's shoulder as she left me and went inside the room. *That could have been us*, I thought. We weren't out of the woods yet, but at least we weren't there.

As I walked, I cried for Denise, for the young man and his father, who had the impossible task of saying goodbye to his young son. I cried for everyone on the floor, each facing their mortality or that of a loved one.

I stopped in the windowed hallway and looked out at the city. I allowed the tears to flow freely and let them pepper my shirt with wet dots of sorrow.

"Please don't cry, Mags. We're okay," Luke said, pulling me in for a snuggle, with Richard the chemo caddy lurking behind him, sending poisons into the veins of my loved one.

21

THE NEXT DAY LUKE ASKED FOR A GRINDER from Jimmy John's. It was clear he was at least trying to feel better, so I was happy to get one for him and one for myself for lunch before my two o'clock pitch for a corporate reality show hybrid that could be the next step in my career.

When I got back with the sandwiches, Luke was asleep. I put his lunch on his tray and set up my hospital office on the second cart. I didn't want anything to ruin this possibly massive opportunity with a brand-new client, Jenn.

Headphones on and ready, I dialed into the call, glad that my technical team was on the line to show how we could technically support my idea. This project was worth a million dollars.

After Jenn logged in and there was a round of introductions, I gave a quick spiel about Heroic Video. She explained that they were looking for a fresh idea, one that did not get pitched constantly. I told her about *Maven*: We would lock three social media mavens in a room for two weeks. We'd give them a new account on their social media platform, Spark, and within four days, they'd have to organize a flash mob in a country they'd draw out of a hat on Day One. "It would show how a connected maven grows a community of net new followers," I finished.

"I like it," she said. "But how does it work?"

Our technical advisor, Mike, and I helped her understand the logistics. I could hear tapping keys as she said, "Brilliant, and how much would this cost? Can you get me an estimate by Friday?"

Suddenly, my headset died. I pulled it off and immediately transitioned to the computer microphone. I didn't want to wake Luke up with the noise from my meeting, but he'd understand if I did.

"Sorry, my headset died. Can you hear me?"

"No problem," Jenn said. "I was asking for an estimate by next Friday. Is that possible?"

"Absolutely." I paused. Luke got up from his bed and groggily dragged himself to the bathroom. "I'll put together an estimate and"—Luke hadn't shut the door. He let out a huge fart and started to pee. I cringed but hoped my computer microphone wasn't good enough to catch the sounds—"put together a plan for how this show will highlight how cool Spark is." *FLUSH*. Everyone paused.

"Great!" Jenn said. "I can't wait to hear from you."

We said our goodbyes and got off the call. Luke was already back in bed, sound asleep. I immediately called Mike. Before he could even say hello, I blurted out, "How much of that did you hear?"

Mike began to laugh. I could hear Josh, a technical producer, laughing in the background.

"Sorry," Mike said, continuing to laugh.

"Just the flush?"

"Not exactly."

Oh god! They'd heard the fart, the peeing, and the flush. Great. "Well, I guess that's a great way to make a first impression." I felt mortified. How could I have blown this pitch? *Stupid, stupid, stupid,* I muttered to myself. What was I going to do to save this potential client relationship?

LUKE WOKE UP and took a few sips of water before rubbing his tired eyes. He looked over at me, noting the flush on my face. "What happened?"

"What happened? Really? Did you not notice I was on a call? All you had to do was shut the bathroom door, and the sounds of peeing, farting, and flushing wouldn't have made it to my potential client in California!"

"Sorry. I was still half-asleep."

"Why didn't you shut the bathroom door?"

He shook his head. "Dunno, I was tired, and I get sick of dragging Richard everywhere. If it's open, he can stay outside the door."

"Never mind," I grumbled.

"Hey, don't you get mad at me. I'm stuck here. If you want some privacy, Mags, you can work in the family room or elsewhere. I'm tired, I'm sick of this," he said, shaking the tubes around. "So, give me a break here, huh?"

"You're right. Sorry. I just really want this client and am not sure what to do. My idea for the *Maven* show could be the next substantial step in my career."

"I know. I know. Just tell Jenn the truth."

"That means I tell her you have cancer. Isn't that using the cancer card?"

"I'll give you a pass. A one-fart pass," he said, laughing weakly at his joke. I tried to stay mad, but I couldn't help but laugh.

LATER THAT DAY, Luke wanted to do his laps. Around the floor we went, fighting the urge to peek into each room.

In one, I saw an empty bed. Sheets were bright white, pulled tight, waiting for the next patient. My heart sank. That was the same bed that Denise's friend had been in just a few days ago. He was gone. Luke had continued walking ahead of me and was now waiting by the windows up the hallway. A nurse stopped and asked if I needed anything.

"The young man who was in that bed. Where is he?"

"I'm sorry," she said. I knew what that meant. I walked to join Luke.

"Hey, look, you can see the flag on top of the Space Needle. They've replaced the American flag with the Seattle Storm flag. They sure have been winning a . . ." He saw the tears streaming down my face. "What happened?"

I pointed back at the room, sucking in a deep breath. He grabbed me and held me tight.

THAT SATURDAY, we were especially grateful to leave this floor and get back home to our life, as different as it was now. At least we'd be with our fur baby. As usual, Luke was packed and ready to go. I had watched him that morning as he dragged himself around the room, slowly folding his dirty clothes and putting them in bags. He searched the room at a snail's pace, ensuring that neither he nor I left anything behind.

When the nurse came and discharged us, he jumped to his feet. "Okay, let's go."

I asked him to stop.

"Right, you like to take these photos of me leaving the hospital. I don't know why, but you do." He stopped and gave me a thumbs-up with a weak smile. "That good enough?" he asked, not waiting for the answer before continuing to the elevators.

He held the door for me, and I stepped in. "Everything okay?" I asked.

"I'm just done. I want to be at home."

Again, we rode home in tense silence.

22

FROM THE DRIVEWAY, we could see Westy's nose pressed against our house's window. Luke looked over at me, confused.

"I don't know," I said.

As we got out of the car and collected the bags, the front door opened. Westy came bounding out to the sidewalk, wiggling and wagging all over the place and dropping sloppy kisses anywhere her tongue could reach. Ronnie stood in the doorway with a glass of wine and a big smile. This made me suspicious.

"Welcome home, party people. There's some wine in the fridge and a fresh lasagna for you to bake tonight."

"Thank you?"

"Luke, you look like you're moving pretty slow. You okay?"

"Yeah, just tired," he said, brushing past her to land on the couch. I followed him in, and Ronnie tagged along behind us. She patiently waited while Westy greeted us with more kisses and grumbling as if she was telling us about her day. When Westy finally settled at Luke's feet, I turned to Ronnie, who handed me a glass of wine. "Cheers!"

I clinked her glass and took a sip of wine. "Okay, what is this about, Ronnie?"

"Why so suspicious?" she asked with a twinkle in her eye. "Okay. So, I spoke to Lachelle, and she said she would get me a discount on a suite at the Four Seasons."

"That's great!"

"With one small caveat."

I shook my head. "I'm listening."

"That next Tuesday, we watch her kids for an hour while Lachelle settles a few things with her attorney."

"Divorce? How do you, Miss Matchmaker, feel about that?" I asked.

"Hey, I can match them, but it doesn't mean I help with the whole relationship. She got a new job, he was pissed about it, they fought, and boom, divorce."

"That's sad. I thought they were cute. Wait, 'we'? Why are 'we' babysitting? I'm not the one that needs a suite?"

"She may think I'm not fit to watch them on my own. No deal without you. Please? Pretty, pretty please." She dropped to her knees, squeezing my hands.

"Fine," I grumbled. "Don't say I never do anything for you."

I DECIDED TO GO INTO THE OFFICE on Tuesday morning instead of working from home. I wanted to see my assistant, Etta, and find out if she had learned anything about the pitch.

I walked into our converted sixties fire station turned office. Since the team was growing, they took the bay that previously housed fire engines and turned it into office space. We didn't own the place, so we couldn't remodel. Next best thing? Put large cream-colored safari-style tents in the bay, add desks, and voila—office space. Etta and I had desks near one another. But instead of heading directly to our office, I stopped by Mike and Josh's table on the way. They looked up at me and smiled.

"Any news?" Mike asked calmly. Josh began to laugh and made farting sounds with his hands below the table.

"Not funny, man. Not funny at all. This show could put Heroic and our careers on the map."

Josh shook his head. "Sorry, Maggie. I make jokes when I'm nervous. I want to see *Maven* be a real hit too. But that was a pretty impressive fart." He chuckled again.

My head dropped to my chest. "I know. I know. But let's focus on getting that pitch deck and estimate to her by Friday. Okay?"

"You bet," Josh and Mike said in unison.

The next stop was my office. As soon as I cleared the opening to the tent, Etta bounded out of her seat and threw her arms around me like she was gathering the most glorious flowers.

"How is Luke?"

"Good, he's home now. He's resting today, so I thought I'd check in. Any word from Jenn's assistant?"

"Not a word. Want me to follow up?"

"No, let's focus on getting the pitch put together. How is the deck looking?"

"Fantastic, if I do say so myself. It's in your inbox. Let me know any changes you want, and I'll push it through the brand team."

"Super, thanks!" I buried myself in reviewing the deck and changing some of the words. I hoped Jenn could forgive us enough to consider this idea.

THAT NIGHT, Westy was leaping around the house like a crazy dog. She ran from the front window to the back door to the front again.

"Looks like someone has the zips," I said with a chuckle as Westy spun, then skidded out on the carpet, pulling it off the padding into a wad under her feet. She growled and took off again toward the back door. "Maybe, just maybe, a walk is in order?"

"I think so. I'd like to go." Luke smiled.

"Great!" After grabbing the blue Nikes out of the closet, I opened my sock drawer, pulled out a pair, and then closed the drawer as it squealed. Westy heard that noise and tore into the bedroom, sniffing at my shoes, finally grabbing one sock and taking it to Luke in the other room. "Well, that's not going to help me out." I laughed, following her.

Westy was on to us now, rumbling up a storm to show her enthusiasm. I grabbed her leash and hooked her up.

"I haven't gotten to walk her in a long time. Let me," Luke said with a grin. I handed the leash to him and opened the door. He had worked so hard training her that I was happy when she sat down inside the doorway. Luke scanned the street for cats, dogs, anything that moved. Westy still had a strong prey drive; anything could send her into a barking fit. The coast was clear.

"Okay, let's go." With that, she padded out the door and stuck right to his side in a good heel.

I was shocked. "The few times I've walked her, she pulls like an asshole the whole time." Westy looked at me as if she knew I was complaining about her.

"Maybe she was in a rush to see if I was home. My dog training podcast talks all about the pack." He smiled.

I remembered the big, scared fur ball of a rescue dog we'd brought home a little over three years ago. She was so cute and very sensitive from whatever bad situation she had come from. We spent many a weekend in the backyard, taking turns walking her in circles and figure eights, training her to heel. She fought us at every turn, sometimes bounding up in the air and pulling the leash from our hands. Training Westy through her excitement was an area where Luke's patience paid off. I got irritated many times and just dropped the leash, giving up. Luke had her sit and make eye contact to calm down while he rubbed her ears. Then he would start again. I feared she would never get it, but he had a dog that could heel within a few weeks. Not all of the time, but she did well.

The sidewalks were dimly lit by the streetlights, highlighting the sprinkle of rain in the air. I fell back on the second block because an overgrown hedge made the path too narrow for all of us. From behind, they looked so calm and perfect. Westy proudly trotted along next to her dad as he praised her for being a good dog. At the end of the block, he stopped. Westy slowly sat down next to his foot as I caught up with them. Luke's grin was making his whole face glow with pride.

"You did such a great job with her, honey," I said, rubbing his shoulder. He took a step into the street. I hung back again, hoping to get a cute photo of them walking together. I wanted to cherish this moment. Digging my phone out of my pocket, I heard a scream.

"No!" Luke yelled. I looked up, and he was lying on the cement. Westy ran down the street after a black cat, her leash bouncing along behind her. I paused, unsure if I should check on him or chase Westy.

"Go get her!" Luke called out. I broke into a run after Westy, who was now around the next corner. I could hear her barking. In our tall old oak tree, a black cat sat on a thick branch, hissing. I stepped on Westy's leash.

"Leave it. No, leave it, Westy!" I demanded, wanting to rush back to Luke. I pulled on the leash to get her to follow me, but she continued to bark. I gave the leash a harder pull, and she fell in line.

She followed behind me, continuing to turn around to look back at the cat every few steps. "Come on, let's go!"

We rounded the corner, and Luke was still on the ground, holding his knee. I started to run. "Are you okay?" I yelled.

He ignored me and began pulling his pant leg back down. When I reached him, he was pushing himself up.

"Yeah, that just hurt. I want to head home." Without another word, he turned toward the house. I looked down and shook my head at Westy, who wagged her tail.

"I'd yell at you, girl, but I'll bet you don't even remember that cat anymore." She kissed my hand. We rushed to catch up to Luke, who seemed to have a mild limp with his left leg.

"You want me to get the car, Luke?"

"I'm fine. Stop worrying," he said without looking at me.

"Is your knee okay?"

"Yep, I just got a bit of a scrape and a hole in my pants. I should have been able to hold on to Westy, Mags, but I couldn't. My hands just wouldn't grip the leash." He stared at the ground as he walked. "I'm weak. I'm useless."

"Not at all, love. Your body is so busy fighting Arnie. It makes sense you have less strength."

"So you have noticed? I thought so."

"Not really. But I have never heard of five straight days of chemo. The amount of poison you are mainlining right into your veins is terrifying."

"God, I hope this works. I hate being so utterly useless."

"I know, love, I know." Westy fell into line next to Luke, licking his hand as it swung at his side.

THE FOLLOWING DAY, after we both had some caffeine in our system, I decided to finally broach a dreaded subject of conversation: Thanksgiving. It was tomorrow. Luke loved this holiday, but since he was sitting on the couch with an angry pinched-forehead grimace, I was worried about how he felt about Thanksgiving this year.

"Tomorrow night is Thanksgiving, and we haven't even spoken about it. Do you want turkey? What sounds good to you?"

Luke took a sip of coffee, seeming deep in thought. When his parents lived in Seattle, we had gone over there, sometimes with Ronnie in tow. But they'd been gone for a few years now. When they left, we began to attend Friendsgiving.

That first year, we went over to our friend Nancy's and brought Ronnie, who was recently single and pouting. I made my famous pumpkin pie.

Nancy greeted us and took our dish. Friends were lingering in a tiki-style cabana next to their hot tub outside. That night had been fun. We met new people, drank a lot of wine, and slept in their guest room. We had repeated this tradition for the past three years, but there was no invite this year. I didn't want to bring this up for fear of hurting Luke's feelings.

"I guess we're not going to Nancy's?" he asked.

"I'd honestly be afraid to go there because there will be many different people with different germs. I want to keep you safe."

"I'm not some fragile doll, Mags. I have done great so far other than my fall last night, and I'd like to go. Did you tell her no?"

"No." I looked down at my lap. "She didn't ask, but remember, we have been hiding out and not communicating much. I can call her, but that's awkward. She's one of many friends who seems to avoid us for fear of not knowing what to say. What do you think I should do?"

"I say let's just forget it. I'm not up for a bunch of pity. I feel useless enough."

Staring at the floor, I wasn't sure what to say. My head spun with ideas, grand plans that I knew were likely a bad idea right now.

"Wait a second. What if I go to Metropolitan Market and pick up a small dinner with all the fixings and we eat here? We could eat, then watch your favorite movie?"

"You'll agree to let *National Lampoon's Christmas Vacation* play on our screen? I have to take you up on that!" A small smile spread on his face. "That is such a rarity."

"Turkey and terrible movies, what could go wrong?"

"You mean, wonderful, amazing, hilarious movies? Okay, you're on."

I ordered the meal online and sat back, glad we'd resolved the Thanksgiving debacle.

FOR ONCE, I wasn't hungover the day after Thanksgiving. So maybe it wasn't such a bad thing that we'd had a simple, low-key celebration this year. Heck, I even enjoyed Luke's *National Lampoon's Christmas Vacation* movie for once!

Friday morning, even though it was a holiday for most, my team had to work to get Jenn her deck in time. I got on a call with Etta, Mike, and Josh. Together, we reviewed the deck. The budget came to $1.2 million for five episodes. It was a significant risk for Spark, but one that could pay off.

I wrote my email and read it four times before hitting Send. Then, I took a deep breath and shut my computer.

THE NEXT FEW DAYS WERE A BLUR. I tried to keep myself busy while Luke silently watched TV on the couch all day long. He looked so sad. I didn't know what to do to help him. I so badly wanted to talk to him about my pitch, but I feared he already felt guilty. If I didn't get the job, he might blame himself. So I stayed silent about Spark.

Occasionally, I would hear him laugh as he watched all the *Friends* reruns from the early nineties. Sometimes I would join him. Other times I left him alone. But on the third day of his TV marathon, no matter what I did, I could not seem to cheer him up. As he lay there on the couch, not wanting to eat much, I called his mom from my office upstairs.

"Well, hello, dear. Is everything okay? How's my Lukie?"

"He's taking the treatment well, but I'm beside myself. He's so sad, Judy. What can I do?"

"You've sat with him? Told him how proud of him Harlan and I and you are?"

"I have. Luke just rolls his eyes." I paced while we talked. "I'm lost."

"Hmmm. This reminds me of when Luke was a little boy. We had to have his tonsils taken out in the middle of the summer. He pouted on the couch, watching out the window while his friends rode bikes, skateboarded, and played. He did this for nearly two weeks. Then I made my famous chicken noodle soup. He slurped that up with joy, and his throat began to feel better. He asked for another portion of soup for breakfast the next morning. I thought it was an odd request, but I did it. When he finished, he went back to lie on the couch. I called the doctor to see how I'd know when Lukie was ready to get back to his normal play. He said if his coloring looked good, enough time had passed. I walked into the den. Luke looked up, and the sparkle was back in his eyes even though the frown remained. I sent Luke outside to see his friends, warning that I'd bring him back in if

153

he played too hard. He went out and skated around the block once with his buddies. After that, he was tired and came in on his own. He was only out there for five minutes, but it refreshed him and brought my sweet boy back. After that, he slowly joined his friends, building up his busy boy self. He always thought it was the soup, not the rest, that made him better. I'll email you the recipe. I think you should make it for him and remind him of its superpowers."

"Oh my god. That sounds fantastic! Yes, please. I'll try anything at this point, Judy. Anything."

"The secret with this dish—use fresh noodles and fresh dill. I'll send it when we get off the phone."

"Thank you so much, Judy!"

"Now, honey, how are you doing? The cancer treatment has to be awfully hard on you."

"Oh, I'm good. I'm not the sick one. How is Harlan?"

"Dear, caretaking is hard. Harlan continues to get better and better. He's resting well and coughing a lot less. I think we are out of the woods. Thanks for asking."

"How are you, Judy?"

"Aside from missing my babies, I'm doing well. Today I'm going to play bridge with the ladies. I've missed those social events. I need to run soon. Give my boy kisses from his mama. I love you, Maggie. I'm proud of you and all the love and care you give to Luke. I can't imagine how terrible I'd feel being this far from my son if I didn't fully trust his caretaker. You are an amazing woman, and I'm proud to call you my daughter-in-law."

As she spoke, I burst into tears. Even from thousands of miles away, Judy knew how to be an incredible mom.

"Thank you, Mom."

A half hour later, my phone dinged with the recipe for the magical chicken soup. I told Luke I had errands to run.

THAT NIGHT, I brought a cup of soup to Luke as he lay on the couch.

"I'm not hungry, Mags," he said, avoiding eye contact.

"Just take a few bites, and I'll leave you be."

"Come on, can I just eat when I'm hungry?"

"Pretty please?" I said, batting my eyelashes and smiling.

He shook his head with irritation, but he took a spoonful of chicken, noodles, carrot, and a few flecks of the fresh dill floating on the top. Then another.

"Hey, this tastes familiar," he said, staring into the cup. "It reminds me of something. What is it?" He ate two more spoonfuls. "Man, this is good. Thank you, Maggie."

"What does it remind you of? I'm curious."

"Not sure. I can't place it," he said between bites. I sat on the coffee table next to the couch.

"Think about it. I'd love to know what it reminds you of."

"Mags, really?" he asked, slightly annoyed.

"Humor me. I spent all day making it."

"Reminds me of childhood somehow. Wait a minute, is this my mom's recipe?" He took another taste, moving it around in his mouth. "Oh yes, yes, it is, isn't it?" I smiled. "This is a magical soup!" Luke sat up. "My mom made this soup when I had my tonsils removed. Once I got it in my system, I went outside and rode with my friends. It had felt like a year of watching them play while I sat inside. It was torture. No one in Seattle should get surgery in the summer. You need to snag that sun when you can."

Luke looked out at the fading light outside. The sky glimmered in hot pinks and purples. "I think I'll take a quick spin on my board. Do you mind?"

I cringed. I knew Luke's knee was still hurting him, but I didn't want to kill this enthusiasm. "Mind if Westy and I chill on the porch and watch?"

He grinned like a child as he jumped up off the couch and grabbed his board and helmet from the basement.

"Let's do this!" he said, leading our little family outside. He got on his board and rode south down the street.

I sipped a cup of hot tea. Westy sat by my side, grumbling that she was not joining him on the ride. "I know, girl. When he gets better, he'll take you with him again," I said to her with a laugh. It had been a long time since his last ride on the electric skateboard.

After going around the block, Luke's cheeks were flushed with the cold and joy. Westy's tail swept back and forth as he walked up the path to the house. When he stopped, Luke called out, "Okay girl." Westy charged off the porch and ran around him, whining and barking in celebration.

OVER A WEEK AFTER THE *MAVEN* PROPOSAL WENT IN, an email from Jenn popped into my inbox. My hands began to shake. This was the moment. My career could finally be moving up.

> Maggie,
>
> Thanks for your detailed proposal. Looking at the materials, it seems like Heroic Video's key strengths don't entirely overlap with the vision we have for this project. Thanks again for taking the time to put this proposal together for us.
>
> Best wishes,
> Jenn

My stomach clenched. Could it be that we weren't a good fit, or was this all because of the snafu in Luke's hospital room? I took a deep breath and emailed my team an update.

I closed my computer. I needed to do something to distract myself. Cookies.

As I was pulling all the ingredients out, Luke came into the kitchen to refill his water. He looked over at my face, flushed from crying.

"Mags, what's wrong?"

"We didn't win the Spark bid. It's fine. I'll get over it." I shook my head and continued pouring flour, sugar, and milk into the bowl.

Luke came up behind me, pulling me close. "You don't think it was my fart routine that lost it for you, do you?"

"That would be pretty shallow," I said, not exactly answering the question.

"Maybe you should call her and get more details. It's worth a try."

"Maybe. I just don't want to seem like a sore loser." I focused on my cookies.

THAT SUNDAY NIGHT WAS CHEMO EVE. I had discovered a new Ethiopian restaurant just a mile from our house. Luke was not adventurous, but he would try new cuisines with me. I looked at their menu online, grinning with the memory of the first time I'd exposed Luke to Ethiopian food. We had only been dating for a few weeks, and he told me he liked to eat with his hands. I'd figured this was a perfect introduction to a cuisine where that is all you do. I took him into the international district in Seattle for his foray into a new set of flavors. I ordered my favorite—kitfo—some meat, and a vegetarian platter, and the meal was delicious. Luke politely ate the meal and did admit the food tasted good—even my raw beef. I felt like the evening was a success. Unfortunately, two days later, we learned that the health commission had shut the restaurant down for health code violations. Whoops. Since then, Luke being a germaphobe, we always checked the health ratings before eating out.

I was reading the new restaurant's menu when Luke came up behind me. "What are you doing?" He peered at my screen. "Ah, you thinking about Chemo Eve? Want to try this place?"

"Ah, it's okay, love. We can do that later. What are you craving?"

He grinned. "A happy wife and some raw beef—the safe kind, that is. You made my magic soup, so let's get you something special."

"You sure?"

"Yup."

"Okay, count me in!" I jumped up and hugged him tightly.

23

THE ELEVATOR DOORS OPENED ON MONDAY MORNING, revealing the ONCOLOGY sign to which I was growing accustomed. For the first time, I noticed the distress marks on the metal letters. It gave them a kind of sparkle that I had missed during my previous visits. Maybe this signified more than the fear, loss, and utter horror of learning someone you love has cancer. Maybe the sign and its slight sparkle showed how we could get through this, or at least try with the help of the fantastic staff on this floor. Maybe this sign stood for hope, help, and possibility. Just maybe? I thought it over for a moment, realizing that this shifting perspective could be an option for me.

For chemo round number five, we got a corner room, neither big nor small, just okay. My cot fit in there, and there was space outside the room where I could stash it, folded up, during the day. It worked and it worked well.

Luke lay on the bed, waiting for the chemo to be mixed and delivered. He was currently getting steroids. I put the sterilizing foam on my hands inside the room and rubbed. Luke stared at me with crazy eyes and a sneaky grin.

"Before you got up here, I managed to get one of the Richards with the purple wheels. I think they are faster. Maybe we can race Ming if she's here."

Luke kicked back on the bed and turned to the window. Outside, it was raining hard. We could see the large droplets bouncing off the rooftops below our room. Looking straight out, we could see a few cranes, busy building a skyline that in a few years would be entirely new. We both gazed at the city for a few moments.

"You ever been to dinner up there?" he said, pointing at the top of the Columbia Center tower. "That's my favorite building. Someday, I'd like to eat up there."

"Yeah, that would be neat. Isn't it some private club or something?"

"I think so—kind of like the Rainier Club. But I'd bet we could find help getting a reservation. You think?"

"Sure! I bet we could." As we watched, planes lined up, heading toward the airport. I longed to be up in the air, on vacation instead of here in the hospital. I sighed.

"Dreaming of trips, Mags?"

"You're on to me. I would love to be flying somewhere warm—a cool breeze blowing across us as we lay in a beach cabana drinking tropical cocktails. 'Margaritaville' would play on some speakers as we soaked up the sunshine. Then you would get up and beg me to play the waves with you."

"So, you haven't thought about it much?" Luke laughed. "You know you could take Ronnie and go."

"Like that would be relaxing!"

"Excuse me!" a voice came from the doorway. Luke and I turned from the window to find Ronnie standing just inside the room. "Why wouldn't it be relaxing if you were with me?" Her tone was off. I knew that she was trying to be playful, but the grit in her voice told me she was mad.

As she entered the room, two nurses came in with Luke's first bag of chemo. They compared his bracelet and number to their records, confirming it with one another, always double-checking that he was getting the correct medication. Ronnie paused to watch this whole process.

Ronnie abruptly turned to the nurses. "Are you guys, like, that unsure? Or did one of you make some kind of blunder and kill someone?" She turned to me. "Doesn't this kind of thing make you nervous? I mean, good god, that's horrifying."

"Ronnie, this is the protocol for everyone. Not just here. It's a safety measure." To the nurses, I said, "Sorry, my sister clearly has a disorder where she blurts out whatever runs through that crazy head of hers."

The nurses laughed, checked a few things on Luke, and left the room.

"What's up, Ronnie?" Luke said, staring over at her red spike heels and tight black dress. "Seems like you're dressed nice for a gal going to a place that creeps you out."

"Ewww, it does, but I needed to talk to you two. I was just down at the Four Seasons looking at the room I got when Devan called. He may not be able to come! Can you believe that? Apparently, it's just a scheduling issue, but he's not sure when he will be able to make it. What do I do? I mean, this guy was totally in love with me less than a year ago. Here I am giving him the opportunity of a lifetime, and he's blowing me off. I mean, really. Blowing ME off!"

"Maybe he's just not that into you anymore, Ronnie—did that occur to you? It has been a while," Luke said, lowering the back of his bed so he could sleep.

"There is no way he got over me that fast."

"Stand up for yourself, Ronnie," I said. "Just tell him which days you're free and if he can't make it, you're moving on. If you just lay down the law, you can determine if he's still into you. That would be my suggestion."

"Well, sure, that may work. But, Mags, I thought maybe you could take some photos of me and post them on Facebook. Are you still friends with Devan on Facebook? You could even tag him in it. Pretend that you think he's still coming and say you're excited to see him. Oh . . . or maybe you could post, Luke. You could take a picture of the two of us together and note how helpful I've been and how happy you are to have such a great wife and sister-in-law." She nodded, pleased with her plan. "We should do all of that. If he sees a new photo, it'll remind him how much he used to love my legs." She extended her leg, twisting it from side to side, showing off the perfectly tanned skin.

Luke rolled over, turning away from her, and closed his eyes. "I'm not using Facebook anymore, Ronnie, so I'm out."

Ronnie pouted and turned to me. "Come on, Mags, will you do it? Pretty, pretty please?"

"It's so immature, Ronnie. Why don't you give my suggestion a try?"

"Okay, I'll do that . . . if you post a picture of both of us and tell Devan you're looking forward to seeing him. Please, please, please."

"Fine, Ronnie, but I want to note I'm doing this under protest."

"That's okay. Luke, can you take the picture?" She looked over at him. He began to snore. I had to hold back a laugh, sure that he wasn't asleep.

"Let's let him sleep, Ronnie. Why don't we do a selfie in the large paned window in the hallway?" We walked out of the room and down the hall to a spot with good lighting. Ronnie reached her long arm up and snapped a few shots. She reviewed them, flipping between them. "This one, I like this one."

In the photo, my mouth curled up like I was the Joker. "Can we use one where I don't look like a weirdo?"

"Oh, now who's being immature? Fine." We got back into position, and she snapped one more at a high angle, kicking her leg out in front of her, making sure it made an appearance in the photo. She examined the photo, then gave a thumbs-up in approval. "I just sent it to you. Let's go into the family room so you can post it before I leave."

We sat down on the couch I've shared with Becca numerous times, and I wondered how she was doing. I wanted to go find her. Instead, I posted the photo, tagged Devan, and played along with Ronnie's plan. "There. You happy? I feel like such an idiot."

Ronnie ignored me and grinned. Leaning over, she wrapped her arms around me. "Thank you so much! I know this will work. You'll see. I'm going to get going. Say goodbye to Luke for me?"

WHILE LUKE SLEPT, I felt antsy. I decided to take a walk. I peered out the hallway windows. Was it warm enough to walk outside? Behind me, a man's voice increased suddenly in volume, getting close to a yell.

"She killed her. Do you hear me? She killed her!" the man exclaimed, pointing inside a room. I went over and saw Becca's mother covered in a white sheet. Becca's head rested on top of the sheet while she sobbed.

Lara was busy trying to calm this man down. I slid past them and into the room. I knelt on the floor next to Becca.

"Hey, I'm sorry." She leaned in close. I embraced her.

"She's gone." Becca pulled back to look at me with bloodshot eyes. "She's really gone."

The chaos continued outside of the room. I heard color codes ringing through the halls from the hospital speakers. I was betting that one was to security to remove this angry man.

"Do you want to stay or take a walk?" I asked.

Becca looked at the sheet and back to me. "The hospital is going to come to get her in an hour. Let's walk. I want to get away from my dad."

"Killer! Murderer! I'm calling the cops."

"You know what, Dad, do that. Call them. I dare you." They stared at each other, and then he began to dial his phone.

"Let's go," I said, grabbing her arm.

For a while, Becca and I walked around the block outside in silence.

"She fell. Last night she fell trying to get out of bed. What if I had been awake and stopped her?" It seemed as if Becca had gone from sobbing to stone-faced in one moment.

"You can't be awake all the time, Becca. So be gentle on yourself."

"She's gone. Now my father is alone. It's time for me to stand up to him and move out. Did you hear him accusing me of murder?"

"Yeah, I did." I kicked the weeds popping through the cement with my blue sneaker.

We sat on a cement barrier outside the front lobby of the hospital. "I feel sad. I feel relieved. But I'm also numb." She looked down.

"You're probably in shock. Plus, your dad was pretty harsh. But you did the right thing by your mom. I hope you know that." She crossed her arms and looked away. "Losing parents is awful. When mine passed, the best thing someone told me was, you'll never get over it. You will always miss your mom. But it will get easier to live with it and celebrate the good times."

Becca smiled weakly. "I suppose so. Let's get back upstairs. I want to be there to say goodbye to her body when they come to get her."

Back upstairs, Becca's father was gone. Becca went back into the room and pulled the sheet down. Her mother's face was ashen, but other than the color change, she looked as she had all these months. Becca looked up. "I'd like to be alone," she said. I patted her arm quickly, then walked away.

LUKE WOKE UP TO FIND ME CRYING IN MY CHAIR. He rubbed the crust out of his eyes and began to blink. "What's going on, Mags?"

I blew my nose and wiped my eyes. "Becca's mom," I managed to say before breaking down into heaving sobs.

"I'm sorry. I'm so sorry. How is Becca?"

"Waiting for them to come to take the body. I wanted to stay with her, but she sent me back here."

"She's gotta be in shock."

I paused, taking in every detail of his face. His big brown eyes, weak smile, and kind spirit. "Thank you for fighting. Thank you for staying positive and trying."

"We got this, love. We got this. I may have cancer, but I also have the tools to fight it. Let me go to the bathroom, then let's take a walk around the floor. I don't feel like it, but keeping active may very well be the thing that helps me shake off this nausea."

Once Luke finished in the bathroom, we headed out to do our laps around the floor. When we rounded the corner, we saw Becca and a young man in the hallway. She had nuzzled under his arm in a half hug.

"I wonder if that's her brother," I said.

Luke paused. "Should we give her space and not walk that way?"

Becca looked up and gave us a weak smile. Then she motioned for us to join them. "This is my brother, Justin. Justin, these are my new friends, Maggie and Luke."

The man shook both our hands. "I've heard a lot about you guys. Thanks for helping Becca. Wait, was it you who called me to come back up?"

"Yes, it was. Becca's helped me so much. I'm so sorry to hear about your loss."

"Thank you. I'm glad Mom's out of pain." Becca snuggled into her brother and began to sob loudly. "I'm sorry, sis," he said.

I reached out and rubbed her back.

"Please let us know if there is anything we can do to help," Luke said. "We're here if you need us."

THE NEXT DAY, I couldn't stop thinking about Becca. How was she doing? How was it going with her dad? Did she stand up for herself and tell him she was moving out? I dug through my phone and realized we had never exchanged numbers.

Staring at my phone, disappointed, I began thinking about standing up for myself. Maybe I could follow Becca's lead. Maybe Luke had been right last week. I should call Jenn at Spark and find out why they'd denied our proposal. Before I lost my confidence, I hit the dial button. She answered.

"Hi, Jenn. It's Maggie from Heroic Video. How are you?"

"Oh, hi, Maggie. I'm good. How are you?"

"I'm okay. Thanks for keeping in touch and letting us know you did not select our proposal. If you have a moment, I'd like to hear a bit more about that decision."

"Sure," Jenn said, taking a deep breath. "To be honest, our team loved the idea. It was the most creative approach to responding to our request, but we worried your team didn't have the deep experience needed to pull off something of that scale."

"I see. I think we may have been amiss in not including more about my team's credentials. I worked on reality TV for ten years, just as it began. Mike and Josh also have impressive resumés. Is it too late to discuss it further?"

"We have already engaged another team on their proposal, so I'm afraid it is."

I took a deep breath and decided to take a chance. "I understand. I do want to clear up one more thing about our initial pitch conversation." I sighed, then cleared my throat. "When I last spoke to you, I was in the hospital. My husband has been ill, and he didn't realize you could hear him. So if our lack of . . . couth was a turnoff for you, I can promise nothing like that will happen again."

"I'm not sure what you are talking about," Jenn said.

"Are you sure you didn't hear a toilet flush?" I asked.

Jenn laughed. "Okay, maybe I did hear something. I understand. Is your husband okay? What's he in the hospital for?"

"He's doing okay. He's pretty private, so I'd rather not get into the details. I just wanted to be sure we didn't lose out on doing a great project together just because of that."

"You know what? We're already in motion with this project, but Spark was very interested in *Maven*. So why don't you update your proposal and include details on your team members' work on similar projects? I'll see what I can do."

"Really? I would love to do that. Thank you so much, Jenn! I appreciate the second chance."

"No promises, but I'll see what I can do." I could hear her smile in the tone of her voice.

"Understood. Thank you."

I ran back to Luke's room, excited to tell him the news. But he was sound asleep, and I didn't want to bother him. Back in the family room, I called my team.

"We got another chance with Spark, guys!" The team cheered over the speaker.

MY EXCITEMENT FADED as I watched my husband struggle as the days passed. Luke battled nausea more and more. Each day, I sat at my makeshift desk writing blog posts and calling potential clients. Between work duties, I'd retrieve another can of ginger ale, the only thing that seemed to give Luke relief.

When night came, I sat on the edge of Luke's bed, rubbing his back. "Anything I can do for you, love?"

He quietly mumbled, "No, thanks, love. I just want to sleep."

"Nancy, Veronica, and the girls said they'd come to meet me for dinner near here. Do you mind if I do that?"

He shook his head. I kept rubbing his back until his breathing slowed to a soft snore.

BY THE TIME I ARRIVED AT WITNESS, eight of my girlfriends were already seated, each with a bright-colored cocktail. Nancy noticed me first and leaped to her feet.

"Mags! I'm so sorry." She held me tight. "I'm so, so sorry." Each of the girls got up and gave me a massive hug before taking a seat.

"Okay, ladies. I want one night off. Let's forget about the cancer talk and just pretend things are normal. Can we do that?"

"On one condition," Nancy said. "Can you tell us how Luke is doing?"

I ordered myself a negroni, then I told the girls that it seemed like the chemo was taking well, but Luke was feeling pretty weak and tired.

"To Luke, and many more healthy decades."

With that toast, we finished up all conversations about hospitals, cancer, and illness, focusing instead on lighter topics and our food. Before Luke got sick, I ran a girls' dinner group and for over three months had talked about trying Witness, a cute little Southern restaurant on Broadway not far from the hospital. We ordered another round of cocktails, fried chicken and waffles, shrimp and grits, hush puppies, jambalaya, and crawfish etouffee, and shared it all. It was terrific to get a taste of each dish. My favorite, in the end, was the jambalaya. As we finished up the last bits of the jambalaya and etouffee, washed down with even more cocktails, the server came to our table and laughed when she saw we had almost licked the plates clean.

For dessert, we ordered a last round of drinks and two bread puddings, my favorite dessert. Ronnie regularly made it for me on my birthday because it was easier than your traditional cake and it tasted good. Witness's version was amazing, better than Ronnie's for sure—not something I would ever admit to her.

After that, we called ourselves officially stuffed and promised that we would do this again before too long. As I began to stand, the room spun around me. I realized that I was not merely tipsy. I stumbled backward, catching myself before I fell into the window. The girls laughed at my clumsiness as we each ordered a Lyft.

HALF AN HOUR LATER, I walked into Luke's room. He was up watching the ten o'clock news.

"Well, howdy, partner," I slurred, stumbling into the room, then falling back onto the recliner on wheels. It rolled backward and slammed into the wall with a *boom*. I laughed loudly. "Whoopsie doodle."

"Mags. You're drunk."

I pointed to my nose. "Ding, ding, ding, you're right." I rolled the chair forward and got to my feet. I rummaged around in my bag for my pajama pants and top. When I finally found them, I turned to find the quiet male nurse behind me, checking on Luke.

"Hey! You're the nice one. You're so quiet. What's your name?"

"Sam," he said, smiling at me. "I'm Sam." He turned and went back to get a blood sample from Luke.

"I just want you to know, you're a nice one. We always feel safe when we see it's you on the night shift. You're amazing. You come in and keep Luke safe. You make sure all the tests get run. You do all of this all night long. All while we sleep, and you test things. You're the nice one. You make us feel safe."

"Thank you."

"So safe. We're so lucky to be so safe."

"Enough, Mags!" Luke snapped.

Sam finished up his tasks. "You have a good night," he said as he left the room.

I plopped onto the recliner, sending it reeling into the wall again.

"Fuck, Mags, really? Stop it."

I began laughing again. "You need to relax, man. Really. Just relax. I'm fine. I just need to put my pants on." I kicked my feet up into the air while peeling my jeans off. Tossing them to the side, I pulled the pajamas on.

Luke changed the channel to the movie *Dirty Dancing*. I danced and stumbled all over the room before falling to the floor. I lay there, laughing for a few minutes. Then I began dancing again and fell onto the bed, elbowing Luke in his sore knee.

"Just stop!" Luke yelled.

Sam entered the room again.

"Sam! You're back! Look, honey, it's Sam! He's so good."

"Yes, Mags." Turning to Sam, Luke said, "I'm sorry."

Sam chuckled as he put a cup filled with soda crackers on Luke's tray, along with a pitcher of ice water and a glass. "She may need this."

"Probably," Luke said, shaking his head. Sam left the room. "Maggie. This is so embarrassing. You can leave, but I'm stuck here for another two days. So now I'm the cancer patient with the drunk wife. What were you thinking? I don't care that you went out with your girlfriends and had a good time, but you didn't have to bring your drunk ass back here. I'm sick. Did you know that? I don't feel well and don't want a drunk woman blathering on about nothing in my room."

"You want me to go?" I asked feeling sick to my stomach. "I can go."

"I don't know what I want," Luke said, turning to the TV.

"I'm sorry," I said, leaning back into the chair.

THE FOLLOWING DAY I HAD A POUNDING HEADACHE. I chugged the cold liquid, filling my glass over and over again, grumbling.

"How are you feeling?" Luke asked through tight lips.

"Physically I feel like hell, but I also feel terrible for my bad behavior." I looked at the ground. "What can I do to make it up to you?"

"Now I'm the idiot stuck on this floor with a drunk wife. You can always go home. But I'm stuck."

"I know, honey. I'm sorry. I promise I'll never do that again. Was I awful?"

"No. You don't remember?" Luke asked.

"It's a little blurry. But I remember talking to Sam and finally learning his name."

"Yup. You were a bit over the top."

My face blushed. "I'm sure."

"Mags, I know you are stressed out. So am I. But we are going to get through this together. I just ask that if you feel an urge to get drunk, you take yourself home to do it. I'm embarrassed, but I also get it."

I leaned down and gave him a peck.

"Maybe you'd go get me a donut?"

I rushed to get my jacket. "I'm on my way."

Outside, the rain was falling hard. I pulled my coat up over my head and ran down the sidewalk as quickly as possible to avoid the Seattle soak. I was almost to the donut shop when I heard a familiar voice calling out.

"Ma'am, ma'am, can you help me?"

I turned to find Queenie, the woman who lived in the bus stop shelter. I joined her under the cover.

"I recognize you," Queenie said, smiling and revealing a few missing teeth. "Can you get me some food, please?"

"Of course. I'm going into the donut shop. What would you like?"

"I'd like two apple fritters, a maple bar, and a hazelnut latte with half-and-half."

"What about Bob? Do you think he'll want a donut again?"

The woman looked down, and a few tears streamed down her weathered cheeks. "He died."

My heart sank. I wasn't sure what to say, so I said the only thing I could. "I'm so sorry."

She nodded, looking down at her gnarled hands that fumbled with the hem of her coat.

I wanted to hug her or comfort her somehow, but I didn't get any indication she wanted to be touched. I waited a moment to see if I would find one. When she didn't look back up at me, I figured I should just go and get her donuts.

I went inside the shop thinking about getting myself a treat too, but the idea of losing a companion made me ill. When I saw Queenie a few weeks ago, she seemed a lot happier, but now the sadness radiated from her. No friend, no one with whom to share a donut. All alone. Dining alone could be my future too. It made me grateful for my Luke and the hope we had as he went through treatment.

Inside, when it was finally my turn in line, I placed my order, adding a coffee and a maple bar for myself at the last second.

Outside, Queenie sat in the shelter, still crying over the loss of her friend. I brought the donuts and coffee over to her.

"Would you mind if I join you? I'm Maggie."

Queenie looked up and smiled. "If you want to. But don't you be a do-gooder and try to rescue me. I do just fine on my own, ma'am."

"I understand. I would just like a little company if that's okay with you. Do you want to talk about what happened to Bob, or would you rather talk about something else?"

"When I was a little girl, my mother died. I was so angry. I couldn't understand why my mom had cancer and died when the other kids got to keep their moms. I always felt left out. This losing someone is nothing new. I've done it a million times, and I'm guessing I'll do it a million more until it's my time. I'm okay, lady, really."

"I lost my mom when I was a teenager too. Both my parents were in a fatal car accident when I was seventeen. Thankfully, I had a sister who took care of me. She was only twenty years old, but she took me in. I felt lucky for that. I would have had to go into the foster system otherwise."

"You don't want that. I had a good foster family at first, but then due to a bunch of changes, I had to get moved around." Queenie took a hefty bite of her apple fritter and a swig of her coffee. A loud gasp of enjoyment escaped her lips. "I sure do love these special lattes. Hazelnut reminds me of cookies my mom made."

I sat with Queenie for about half an hour while she shared memories of a fun childhood on Whidbey Island. It sounded ideal until her mother's death left her alone to find her way in the world. She didn't expand much on how she'd become homeless, but I didn't care. Listening to her made me realize that I was the flawed one. I had judged her. Until this moment, I had spent more time thinking about the dirt on her face and clothing than the circumstances that brought her to live in this bus shelter. I was ashamed of myself.

"I enjoyed speaking with you, Queenie." I smiled. "But I need to get back to my husband."

"How is he? Is the treatment going well, Maggie?" she asked.

"Yeah, so far so good."

Queenie patted my arm and squeezed. "The pain only means you truly love."

I smiled before turning out into the rain. I rushed to Luke with his donut in hand.

"Did you stop and get a couple of drinks? The hair of the dog? You look a lot better," Luke teased.

"Very funny, mister. Very funny. I ran into Queenie again, and it was pretty sobering talking to her." Luke listened as I shared her story. "In the end, it dawned on me that I don't want to be a judgmental person. I want to respect that we don't know what someone else is going through. I want to be kind, not some privileged jerk running around, making my perspective the only one I can see."

"Then don't be that person. Honestly, Mags, you are being a bit harsh on yourself. You did take the time to talk to Queenie."

"Will you call me out if I'm being a turd?"

"You bet, Mags. Have I ever held back?"

THE NEXT DAY, Luke looked paler than he had the day before. I put my hand on his forehead as he slept. He seemed to have an average temperature. Worry still crept through my mind like morning glory, its growing tendrils trying to strangle my hope. I didn't want to lose Luke like Queenie had lost Bob. Sure, things were going well, but my folks' accident had taught me that change could come out of nowhere and completely alter the course of my life. My stomach hurt. I tried to appreciate Queenie's message that this pain meant to love.

Finally, it was Break Away Saturday, freedom time. As Luke finished his final chemo bag, we took a walk. Luke was dragging his heels making a slow swishing sound with his shoes but picked up the pace once we saw Ming. Today she wore a brilliant red velour sweatsuit with green embroidered leaves sporting purple blooms. As usual, she had her matching purse. I was so curious about what she had in there. She saw us coming and made a small bow with a big grin as we passed her.

I stopped and turned around. "May I ask you something?"

She paused.

"What do you have in your purse?"

Her smile grew even more prominent. She opened the tiny bag and pulled out a stack of photos and a small dragon figure. "Ya Zi from daughter," she said, pointing to the dragon. "Family with me always."

I grinned.

"I beat and go home for the new year," Ming said.

"Yes, that's perfect. Thank you for sharing."

She bowed and turned to continue her walk.

Like many patients, Ming didn't have visitors, but that didn't make her feel hopeless. She carried her family—a source of hope—with her.

After we finished our walk, Luke began to pack his bags while I looked up the dragon on my laptop.

"You want to know what that figure represents? Ya Zi, the protector dragon god, is a fierce warrior that's always victorious in war. I guess her family sees this battle and gives her the energy to win. Wow. That's cool."

"Sure is."

His bag beeped, signifying the end of its contents. Round five of chemotherapy had met its end. One less battle left in this war.

24

LUKE AND I WERE CURLED UP TOGETHER ON THE COUCH, enjoying the luxury of being at home, when Westy ran to the door, barking. I opened it to find a small package with a card sitting on the porch.

"Any idea what this could be or who it might be from?" I asked Luke as I brought it back to the couch.

Luke shook his head. I opened the tiny package. Inside was a small brooch of a partridge in a pear tree. The card said:

It's Christmas time
We wish you well
Santa sent us
Twelve little elves

We plan to sneak up
And leave you a gift
All to help
Your spirits lift

So keep an eye out
On the stairs at your house
Because we little elves
We are as quiet as a mouse

Merry Christmas
And a happy new year
We're glad you're our neighbors
We welcome you here

Luke turned over the brooch and noticed a small note attached to the bottom: *Look on the side of your house.*

Luke bounded out the door, surprising me with his energy. In a couple of minutes, he walked in with a Harry & David box of pears.

"How nice!" He peeled the gold foil wrapping off one pear and took a bite. "Delicious."

I grinned. Since returning home, Luke had not eaten. Nausea had kept him lethargic. This surprise treat from our neighbors was extraordinary. Just seeing the box on the table made me feel special.

"You think this means they're going to come every night, doing 'The Twelve Days of Christmas'?"

"I do believe so," Luke said, wiping the juice from the pear off his chin. "I can't wait to see what's next!"

THAT MONDAY, I joined Luke for his post-chemo checkup. Waiting for the results, I looked at the artwork covering the walls—what appeared to be intentionally blurry photographs. I caught Luke staring at them as well.

"I didn't feel too nauseous until I looked at those," he said. "They seem like an interesting choice for a bunch of nauseated cancer patients."

The nurse entered the room.

"Luke's counts are low. Not low enough to need a transfusion, but low enough that we need you to be careful."

We nodded in unison.

"I know it's the holiday season, and you may feel that going to a party is okay, but think twice, please."

We agreed and left the office.

Once we got in the car, Luke turned to me. "No white elephant party at Nancy's, huh?" He pushed his lip out in an exaggerated pout.

"I know you love that."

"My spiked eggnog! It's not the holidays without that."

"I'll betcha I can make that happen."

Nancy happily shared her recipe with me, even offering to drop off a batch. I declined, concerned about germs, and she understood.

I took the ingredient list to our usual Safeway. No luck finding the super-secret ingredient, Lactaid soy nog, and vanilla brandy. I drove to the QFC near Nancy's house. Nope. I continued to drive around but none of the shops I tried had any. I had wanted to surprise Luke that night with a fire and this special holiday drink, but I'd failed him.

When I got home, Luke was curled up on the couch watching *Jeopardy!*, his hand hanging over the edge petting Westy. Once she heard me, she bounded over, grumbling in celebration. After putting my purse down and hanging up my coat, I sat on the chair.

Luke looked over at my face. His brow bunched, and his head cocked to the side. "What? What is it?"

"Oh, nothing," I said, avoiding his eyes.

"Seriously, what?"

"I went to five stores to get the ingredients for Nancy's special eggnog, and I couldn't find them all."

"That's okay."

"Yeah, I know, but I thought it would be fun to have drinks tonight."

"I would love to get out of the house. Why don't we do this—I'll drive you around, and you run in and see if you can find everything we need? It'll be fun."

"Don't you want to stay in and have a fire?"

"I've spent enough time on this couch. Let's go."

We grabbed Westy's leash and went out on our adventure. Heeding the nurse's warning, Luke stayed in the car with Westy while I ran into store after store, striking out again and again.

"One more?" Luke asked.

"One more."

We decided to try the QFC in Wallingford, which was a lot smaller than the stores in the suburbs but, being in the city, more likely to have the non-dairy eggnog. I jumped for joy and squealed when I found it. The man standing next to me looked at me like I was an alien. I grinned at him. "You have no idea. I need this."

Next, I went to the liquor aisle and grabbed a nice bottle of brandy. When I got home, I'd slice a vanilla bean, add it to the spiked eggnog, and shake it up. I was dreaming of this tasty treat as I checked out. I could see Luke idling in the parking lot right out front. But I noticed movement near the car. What was he doing? I wrapped up my purchase and went outside.

The man talking to Luke looked at me and smiled as I got into the passenger seat and had my face licked for being gone for too long in dog minutes.

"Mags, this is Johnny. He worked with me at German Automotive."

"Hey, Johnny! Do you still work there?"

"Yeah. We miss Luke." He turned to Luke. "You know you still got a job if you decide to give up that independent stuff when you're back on your feet."

"Thanks, man." Luke reached out and patted Johnny on the arm.

"Okay, I better get back to my old lady. Sorry to hear about cancer, but glad you're starting to feel better."

My head snapped to the side. I looked at Luke, shocked. This was the first time I'd seen him openly admit he had cancer to someone outside of our immediate family. I rubbed his shoulder.

"You told him."

He kept his eyes in front and started the car. "Yep. Not much point hiding my bald-ass head now, is there?"

Even though I was the one shaving the odd-shaped fuzzy growths about once a week, it had not dawned on me that Luke might be recognizable as a cancer patient. So when we got home, I followed him to the house, looking as he walked. His legs were skinny, not as muscular as they'd been during his days as a mechanic. His pants seemed like they might fall off, and his still-broad shoulders had a bony quality to them. I tried to study his face while avoiding detection.

"Mags, you are not sneaky," he said, furrowing his brow. "I know what you are doing."

"I just . . . I just hadn't, really . . ."

He stepped forward and embraced me. A loud sigh escaped his mouth.

"You gonna keep me, Mags?" he asked. "I do look a bit sick."

"I'm keeping you forever," I said, hugging him as hard as I could as Westy pushed her way in between us.

EVERY NIGHT, another elf would sneak up to our porch and leave a gift inspired by "The Twelve Days of Christmas" theme. Some evenings, I'd go out and pick up the treat while Luke slept. Others, he would sit at the window, scaring the neighborly elf away.

On Day Eight, we awoke to a jumbo package on the porch. I was pouring coffee in the kitchen, making my list of groceries to shop for this week, when I heard Luke open the front door. Since the gifts had been a daily occurrence, I wasn't in a rush to discover what this one was.

"Broccoli, steaks, potatoes . . ." I rambled to myself, writing each item in my sloppy cursive/print mixture.

"MOOOOOOOO." Luke stood behind me dressed head to toe in a spandex cow outfit. Little ears attached to a black headband protruded from his bald head. He tossed one hip to the side and gave me a sideways come-hither look. I grabbed my skinny husband and kissed him all over his face, bursting into laughter.

"Tell me you're going to wear that on Christmas when Ronnie comes over? Please?!"

25

WE HAD ALWAYS KEPT our Christmas celebrations small, and sticking to traditions this year was such a welcome relief. Luke and I didn't have to worry about germs or feel left out as we had for Thanksgiving, and I didn't have to cook. It was brilliant. We spent Christmas Eve wrapping the few gifts we bought each other, which were small due to the cost of cancer treatment.

"So, what did you get me? I'm sure you spent a lot of dough. Spill it," Luke teased.

"Uh, yeah, right. I'll bet you had Amazon bring you my gifts?"

"Your gift is ME! You're welcome," Luke said, jumping up and kissing my face. "Truthfully, I didn't get you much. I hope you're not disappointed."

"Love, what I need most is right here: you, me, and Westy." Our dog ran over upon hearing her name, hoping there was a treat in her future. We laughed. "Let's discuss the grand issue for the night."

"What's that?" Luke's brow pinched.

"The Chinese food order for the evening. I think I want stir fry and—"

"I hope this doesn't upset you too much, but I'm not feeling great today, so I may not eat a lot. Order what you want."

With a concerned sigh, I asked, "Would you rather have something else?"

"We'll have white rice, and at a minimum, that should make it down my gullet."

"I'll get your favorite cashew chicken just in case you want some later."

"Sweet."

WITH A HOT PLATE of food in hand and a few dog cookies in my pocket, I settled into the couch next to Luke, my cozy holiday sweatpants with elves on each ankle feeling familiar and festive.

"Oh, I see some cashew chicken on that plate. Feeling better?"

"Yep." He smiled and took a bite. "Just as good as always. Can we start with *A Christmas Story* to complement the Chinese food, then move on to *Elf* and *It's a Wonderful Life*?"

"Sure thing, love!" Westy put her head in my lap and stared up at me. Pulling a cookie out, I asked her, "High five?" She hit my hand with her paw and accepted her prize.

"Before we start, can we talk?" Luke asked, cuing up the movie

"Always." I stuffed a bite of General Tso's chicken in my mouth. "What's up? You want a BB gun for Christmas?" I chuckled, and Luke stared. "What?" I asked more seriously.

"My treatment is so expensive that I'm worried about us. I know our insurance through your job is good, but is it that good?"

"Well . . ." I thought for a moment, deciding if I should make light of the topic or give a serious answer. "Truthfully, we are in good shape. It'll cost us about $15K after insurance for this year and probably less for next year since you'll be finished with treatment in January." I risked a joke. "You know, if you'd planned this better and only had treatment in one calendar year, we'd have less of a deductible to meet. You and planning." I winked.

Luke sighed. "True that. Sorry, Mags . . . But in all seriousness, thank you. I've read that a huge percentage of families need to declare bankruptcy after treatment."

"We're in a good spot, love. I've got this if you do! Managing the money is the easy part. You just kick Arnie's butt to the curb, and we'll be good."

"I'm on it . . . Want a fire?"

"You bet," I said, watching him shuffle to the fireplace, placing one foot in front of the other at a pace that would make a sloth concerned. He started the fire, our tradition for Christmas Eve. A tear of gratitude ran down my cheek as I thought of how lucky we were between his progress thus far and our finances. Not everyone was that lucky.

THE DOORBELL RANG midafternoon on Christmas Day. I looked out the window, and there was my sister in a French maid's outfit. I sighed and opened the door.

"I don't have a lot of money right now, but I wanted to get you a good gift"—Luke appeared at my side—"and . . . make up to Luke for my slightly off-putting behavior at the hospital. So, I'm here to clean!" With the flick of a feather duster, she pushed past us.

Luke followed her as she dusted. "'Slightly off-putting'? I think that's a bit of an understatement."

"Seriously, Luke, take my apology. I care about you and was concerned and very emotional. But I respect that you want a good relationship with the nurses. So I'm here to make up for that, not fight."

"Thanks, Ronnie." He shook his head and went back into the kitchen to start washing and peeling potatoes for dinner.

Time flew by, and it was almost dinnertime. Ronnie grabbed a change of clothes from her car and asked to take a quick shower. Luke and I finished up the mashed potatoes and checked on the roast. Everything was coming out great. I set the table for three, using my angel napkin rings and gold chargers to set the mood.

Ronnie came out of the bathroom made up as if she was going out to a club. Her dress was glittery.

Luke laughed. "We ain't that fancy."

"Hey, you never know what could happen after dinner. Maybe I'll get a call from the Prince of Wales asking me for a date. So it's best to be ready."

"Charles is pretty set up with Camilla," I said. "But, I mean, if Princess Diana didn't grab his attention . . ."

"Hey, hey, hey!" Ronnie stopped me. "Let's not start flinging insults. I want to be ready, just in case!"

"Okay. Well, let's get a cocktail and take a seat in the living room."

A few minutes later, I raised my glass. "To health!"

"And family!" Ronnie added as we toasted. "Thanks, you guys, for giving me the benefit of the doubt and forgiving me for my behavior. I was so stressed out over Devan that I lost sight of what was most important: family. I love you both. You are the only two I can rely on." She raised her glass again. "In fact, you have inspired me! I'm going to donate next year to the pursuit of helping families facing hardships like cancer. I'm not sure how, but I want to be a positive force for good!"

"Hear, hear." Luke smiled. "That sounds like a noble mission, Ronnie!"

"Yeah. Any ideas yet?" I asked.

"A few are percolating, but not anything solid enough to share just yet. I'm doing it for you, for us, and helping."

Three hours later, after dinner, Ronnie's phone rang. "Yup. I do want to get into that field . . . Yeah, I want to talk. When? Tonight? I'm just wrapping up with my family . . . Yes, he is in remission . . . The executive director is going to be where? . . . Do you know him? . . . Yeah, let's talk more about that. See you in about thirty minutes." She turned to us. "Thank you for a lovely evening. You guys are the best. Now, I need to go. This meeting is my first step in figuring out how to change the world. You guys are going to be so proud of me. Next time this year, we'll be toasting the change I have helped bring. You mark my words."

She grabbed her purse and rushed out the door. Luke and I stared at each other.

"I'm so curious, but for now, let's finish our drinks and enjoy the fire."

"Deal!" I said and kissed him all over his face.

LESS THAN A WEEK LATER, on Chemo Eve, Luke and I sat at the front window of our house waiting for a Lyft to arrive and sweep us off to a great night at our favorite bar, Joli.

I grabbed my jacket. "Ready for another delicious—and the final—Chemo Eve?"

Upon arriving at Joli, Matt, the owner, greeted us at the door.

"Good to see you guys again! It's been a while." He led us to one of the enormous wooden booths against a wall decorated with old film reels stuffed with succulents. "You want your usuals? An old-fashioned with rye and a negroni?"

"Yes, sir." Luke smiled.

We began to look over the menu. There were many good dishes to choose from, but our favorite way to dine here was on a Saturday, when happy hour was all day. We'd come in and order nearly one of every appetizer. Then we'd gorge on the chimichurri steak bites, drunken chicken bites, fried green beans, and stuffed olives. By the end of the night, we would barely be able to fit in the donut holes order, but somehow, we always did. Since it was Sunday night, this was not an option. We looked over the menu to find the full entrées that we wanted. A few minutes passed, and Matt was back with our drinks.

"To help you celebrate your final Chemo Eve, I had my cooks make up all your favorite appetizers. I'll have them brought over to you one at a time. Sound good?"

"Sounds great!" I said, trembling so much that I dropped my phone on the ground with a crash. He left, and I turned to Luke. "You told Matt about Chemo Eve?"

"Sure did." He smiled. "Might as well own it. I'm kicking cancer's ass."

"So, this is a card only you can use?" I asked.

"Maybe . . ." He raised his glass grinning like a sly child. We toasted, then gorged on the delicious food as it arrived at the table.

26

RIDING THE ELEVATOR WITH MY COFFEES in hand felt better than it ever had. The bleach and hospital cleaning products didn't smell like impending doom today. I felt good. This was our last trip to the hospital for chemo.

The doors opened, and there they were—those big silver ONCOLOGY letters. I quietly said hello to them. Today, they had no power. All signs pointed to the treatment going well; I could ignore their cold steeliness and continue my journey. As usual, Lara was behind the desk on the phone, smiling. She pointed toward the end of the hall, the room where this whole cancer journey had begun. How apropos—starting and finishing this journey in the same place, but not with the same emotions.

I entered the room, and Luke was busy organizing the space to fit his ideals. I leaped upon the bed, thinking I'd bounce. Instead, I hit a metal bar and laughed, trying to strike a sexy pose. "Hey, handsome, fancy meeting you here."

Luke put on the standard plaid cancer shirt that he had worn each round of this journey. He smiled.

"How are you feeling?"

"Well, they just hopped me up on my steroids and hooked me up. Wanna go see if we can end this with the fastest Richard on the floor?"

"It's the fastest Richard?"

"Yeah, this guy has the mark." Luke pointed at a small purple mark on one wheel. "This one has some fast spinnin' wheels!"

Luke and I tore out of the room in our silly fast walk. We'd done a few laps when we saw a bright blur of mint green in the distance. When we caught up, Ming stopped and turned around. She smiled, waving the hand that held a mint-green purse covered in tiny pink roses. We waved back.

Luke grinned, moved his caddy back and forth, and said, "Zoom zoom." He pointed to her, then back to himself. "Race? *Vroom vroom.*"

She smiled and nodded.

Luke lined up next to Ming, and I put my arms out, using them as makeshift flags.

"Ready, set, go!" I said, dropping my arms. Ming and Luke sped away, hips swinging to get the fastest walk going. Luke was in front for a moment, but Ming got the best of him and launched into the lead as they rounded the corner and I lost sight of them.

They rounded the next corner a few moments later and headed back in my direction. Lara poked her head out from behind the desk and shook it with a laugh. "Hey, you kids need to stop that. It is funny, but seriously."

Ming made it to me first, then Luke. She and Luke were giggling wildly like children.

"Sorry, Lara, but we're done. It looks like Ming won!"

Luke lifted his hand for a high five. Ming met his hand with hers, purse swinging off her arm.

"I would have made it if I hadn't had this," Luke said, pointing to a clump of hair stuck in a wheel. Luke winked at Ming, and she grinned ear to ear. She pointed down the hallway toward her room where a young woman stood. We waved goodbye as she continued her laps.

Luke returned to our room, and I went off in search of a recliner chair I could borrow. As I was rolling one down the hallway, I noticed Becca standing near the nurses' station, dropping off a bouquet of fake flowers to the nurses.

I left my recliner against the wall and ran toward her. When she turned, she smiled and reached out her arms.

"It's so good to see you. How are you?" I exclaimed.

"I'm okay. Things are settling down. I got my apartment, and I love it. But I still miss my mom."

"It hasn't been that long. It should only get better from here. How are your dad and brother?"

"My brother is good. My dad finally realizes that nothing could have saved my mom, so he's coming around. Not that I'm ready to see him."

"I'm glad he sees the truth and you're taking care of yourself."

"How is Luke?"

"He just raced Ming around the loop here, and he lost." I smirked. "So he's a bit bummed out at the moment." We laughed.

A young man came up and put his arm around Becca. She blushed. "Maggie, this is Jack. He's a friend from school who's been helping me move and settle my mom's estate." She looked up at him with bright, smiling eyes. He looked back with complete adoration.

I grinned. "Nice to meet you!"

"We have reservations at Seven Beef in ten minutes. We better go. Nice meeting you, Maggie," he said, shaking my hand. As they reached the elevators, he grabbed Becca's hand and they disappeared.

THAT NIGHT, Luke picked out some of his favorite comedies from the eighties. We had avoided one of our favorites because the name had scared us a bit, and we didn't want to jinx it. But tonight, we celebrated being almost done with *Better Off Dead*. We rolled with laughter as the characters went through a litany of questionable experiences, ones we would never see today. Our favorite part, the very determined paperboy, gets us every time.

Luke turned on the news afterward. I was changing into pajamas when someone entered the room. I pulled my pants up, turning to find my sister. She had crept in on her tiptoes and sat down in my recliner.

Luke and I looked at her, waiting for her to break the silence.

"Devan canceled. He told me to take a hike. It's over." She let out a sigh. "He's done with me. Not sure why he had to drag me along. But I get it. He told me he never wants to see me again."

I stared at her face, trying to read the stony expression. Her tone was uncharacteristically flat. Emotionless. She picked at a chip in her red nail polish.

"I'm sorry to hear that," I said, reaching out to touch her shoulder.

"His loss," Luke chimed in before turning his attention back to the news.

"But this means something great for you two!"

I stared at her.

She waited for Luke to give her his attention. Instead, he watched a five-car pileup on the news.

"Luke? I have a surprise," Ronnie said flatly.

Luke turned to her.

"This is your last treatment, right?"

We both nodded, grins appearing on both of our faces.

"Well, I wanted to treat you to something special. Since I'm not going to use the suite at the Four Seasons, I thought I'd give it to you. I've also included a dinner at the restaurant there."

"Wow, thank you, Ronnie. That's really generous."

"Thanks, Ronnie." Luke smiled.

"You're welcome." Ronnie stood, and I hugged her.

"I'm so sorry, Rons," I said, squeezing her tight.

"Eh, I had a feeling it wasn't going well. I do not beg. Now I'm done with Devan, I can move on." She patted my back and pushed me away. "I'm going to head out. I'll talk to you both later, once you're both done with this god-awful place."

With that, she was gone, just as fast as she had appeared.

Once she was out of sight, Luke turned to me. "I just want to be home, not in a hotel."

"We can save it?" I offered. He nodded and leaned back on his pillow.

A FEW DAYS LATER, it was New Year's Eve. Lara stopped by our room. "Tonight, we will be serving Martinelli's sparkling apple juice and watching the fireworks from the windowed bridge. Will you two be joining us?"

"Of course!" I declared before checking in with Luke. I turned to him and smiled.

"As she said, of course."

We decided to take a walk around the floor for a bit to stretch our legs. Down the hallway, we could see a man standing in a suit. We passed him, noticing he was on a call.

"He's not doing well. I think it's only hours," said the man and paused. I slowed down, curiosity gripping my heart. "Yes, I know the plans. I have the funeral home all lined up. Will you be here tomorrow? Okay, good."

We continued our rounds for about an hour. On our last loop, a rolling bed with posts and curtains all the way around entered the hallway ahead of us. I looked over at Luke.

"We're done," he said, heading back to our room.

Once inside, Luke sat on his bed. "Was that what I think it was?" I asked him.

"Yes, that's probably the guy we heard about."

I peeked out of the room. The man in the suit was following the cart down the hall and into the elevator.

"On New Year's Eve, no less."

Luke wiped a stray tear from my cheek. "Mags, we did okay. We are making it together. Let's use tonight to celebrate our wins, not reflect on where we could have been."

"Agreed!"

That night, we gathered in the hallway by the windows with the best view of Seattle's fireworks. Not only were we surrounded by cancer patients who felt well enough to join us for the juice and view, but there were a few pregnant women as well. I spoke to Jane, who was due to give birth at any moment. With so much death surrounding us, it was refreshing to be sitting next to a pregnant woman about to bring new life into the world. I leaned into Luke, trying to not get tangled in Richard's chemo cords.

We toasted to the night and kissed right at the stroke of midnight. As I lay in bed that night, my heart overflowed with gratitude. I would get to start my new year with my beloved husband and our final trip home.

ON THE LAST MORNING, I opened my eyes to see Luke's empty bed. I looked around, and everything seemed in place. It was odd that he hadn't woken me up. I peered out the door. Down the hall, I could see a lavender velour sweatsuit racing down the hall with Luke. I laughed.

"Couldn't handle losing?" I asked.

"It had to be fair," Luke commented, pointing at the wheel that was now hair free. "But she's still winning."

Ming smiled at both of us, patting our hands. "Safe now. You safe now." She walked away, her little satin purse, filled with her family's love, in tow. I would miss my Ming sightings.

Later that afternoon, Luke was finally unhooked from Richard and given his final dose of steroids.

Luke turned to the chemo caddy to bid it farewell. "See you, Richard. You've been a real dick!"

We packed up our stuff and paused in the doorway. This time, we took a selfie of both of us leaving the room.

Lara appeared. "The tradition is, when you finish chemo, you need to ring the bell. Are you game, Luke?"

Luke smiled. "You bet!"

All the nurses and a few doctors stopped what they were doing and joined hands, creating a tunnel for Luke to run through toward the bell. I rushed to the other side and used my phone to film this moment.

Luke stooped and ran under their arms, passing all these kind men and women who had been there to take care of him, of us, in the most challenging moments of our lives. When he got to the other end, he rang the bell and Lara wrapped her loving arms around him tightly, just as she had the very first night as I had collapsed outside his door. I continued to film until I heard a small choking sound come from him. I knew this preceded crying and he was a private person. I stopped recording. Lara grabbed me too.

All the nurses and doctors on the floor congratulated Luke and thanked him for being such a fantastic patient. "Except for that hall racing. Luke, you're a terrible influence." They laughed and hugged one more time.

As we walked to the elevator, I waved goodbye to the steely ONCOLOGY sign. It was finally over.

Recovery

27

DRIVING HOME FROM THE HOSPITAL felt different this time. We looked at the city in silence, enjoying the fading sunlight. I texted our neighbors to let them know we'd be over shortly to pick up Westy.

As we pulled up, we could hear Westy starting to bark as she smeared her nose across the neighbors' windows, announcing her joy. We unpacked the car and got to the front porch. I turned and noticed Luke looking at the house with pleasure. The neighbors opened their door. His silent moment of appreciation was over.

Luke called Westy, and she came running. He crouched so she could lick his face and race around him in circles. They did this for a moment before she came running to me, weaving herself between my legs, looking for a scratch right at the top of her tail. I complied, and she grumbled a thank-you.

Inside, Westy nosed through her toys to find the perfect ball to bring Luke. As he put things away, she stayed right on his heels, ensuring that he wasn't about to leave her again.

As soon as Luke sat on the couch, Westy rested her face and red ball on his lap. She sat quietly, looking at him adoringly.

Moments like this made me think Westy was more aware than we were of what was going on in our hearts and minds. Occasionally, she'd nose at her ball, then sniff at his chest. He'd gently toss the ball over his shoulder into the dining room. She'd catch it, then bring it right back with a wag, whining for another round.

I fussed around the house. I couldn't quite identify why I felt so anxious, but everything in me sensed something was off. I wanted to get the house clean and sterile, knowing that although he was okay now, we never knew what would happen when the chemo took hold and knocked his immunities down to nearly zero. I scrubbed and scrubbed as if I could wash away any chance of further illness.

"Hey there, wifey, whatcha doing?" Luke yelled out from the other room. "Sounds like you're stress fussing. Why not come in here and sit with me? I promise to not get my poison on you."

"Not funny, honey," I said, continuing to scrub.

"Maybe a little funny. Come on. You're making me nervous."

I took off the green rubber gloves and put them under the sink. "Want a wine or whiskey?" I asked.

"Why not try some wine?" He patted Westy on the head. "I think someone would also like a c-o-o-k-i-e," he added.

I poured us each a wine and joined him on the long white couch that had served as his nap place and sometimes his bed since September. He had crashed there overnight more times than I could count.

Luke held up his glass. "To the end of chemo!" he declared. We clinked glasses.

"What do you want to do tonight, Luke? Do you want me to cook something special, maybe the Thai chili enchiladas or tacos?

Or is that too spicy? Or do you want to go out? Oh, if we go out, we could go to—"

"Slow down there, tiger. I just got home. Dinnertime is at least two hours away. Can I just rest for a minute?"

"Yeah, sorry. Sorry, honey, so sorry."

"And THAT. You have to stop with that. It's just us. Calm down and just sit with me."

I put my feet in his lap for a foot rub. We had spent many hours rubbing each other's feet over the years. I felt guilty accepting this moment of enjoyment but liked it too much to stop it.

"I can almost hear those gears in your head, Mags. I love your cute little feet. Just let me do this."

I took another swig of my drink, leaned back on the couch, and tried to stop thinking.

We were just deciding what kind of takeout to order when Ronnie arrived carrying a backpack and a bottle of wine.

"Surprise! It's me," she announced, opening the door without knocking. "I'm going to watch the house and Westy tonight, and you, my friends, are going out for a night of pure luxury. Pack your bags. Your Uber will be here in fifteen minutes." Ronnie went into the kitchen and uncorked her wine with a pop. I heard the dog cookie jar open and Westy's nails on the floor.

"We appreciate the offer, Ron, and would love to use it another night. But tonight we just got home."

"My bed is all I want, Ronnie," Luke chimed in.

"Their bed is way better than that old creaky thing you use. Isn't it a double? You have a California king awaiting your arrival. You also have reservations at the Goldfinch Tavern for seven o'clock. Now go, get ready." She took another swig of her wine and sat down on the couch. I could hear her changing the channels as Luke and I went into the bedroom.

"What do you want to do?" I asked Luke.

"Let's just go. Fighting Ronnie will be worse than the Four Seasons."

"You sure?"

"Actually, a king bed and some fancy food sound pretty amazing," he said as he began packing his bags. "Hell, let's do it. Don't forget your swimsuit. I'm sure they have a hot tub."

The sky glowed a glorious purple and pink as we arrived at the hotel overlooking the sound.

"Mr. and Mrs. Byrne, welcome. Congratulations on completing your chemotherapy," the person at the front desk said. "We're pleased to have you here tonight. Please get a complimentary drink in the bar while we take your bags to your room."

I cringed and looked over at Luke. He smiled. "Thank you," he said, giving his bald head a rub.

Luke and I found a cozy couch near the windows where we could watch the rest of the sunset over a drink. We leaned back, held hands, and gathered ourselves into the comfortable silence. What with all the phone calls, beeping, footsteps, and announcements in the hospital, we had not enjoyed quiet in a long time—it felt like years. We sipped our wine and listened to soft jazz as the sunshine made its way to bed.

When we finished our drinks, the bellboy arrived. "May I escort you to the presidential suite?"

Once Luke tipped the bellboy and he left, I let out a scream.

"This room is amazing!" Our room on the tenth floor was in the corner of the building, with windows on two sides. The couches faced a fireplace and a clear view of the water and mountains. The biggest bed I had ever seen faced the water, with a wide-open view of ferries passing in the night, bringing people to and from Bainbridge Island.

I ran over to Luke, wrapping him up in my arms. He snuggled in, then moved in for a long kiss.

We made our way downstairs for dinner at the Goldfinch Tavern an hour later. Even in the dark, the view of the twinkling lights across the sound was brilliant. Luke and I ordered our favorite cocktails. When they arrived, we toasted.

"To an unexpected but glamorous evening," Luke said, giving me a wink.

We mainly stayed quiet, enjoying the beauty and silence. The oysters on the half shell were delicious, as were Luke's salmon and my incredible steak frites. We finished the evening off with tiramisu and coffee.

"Shall we head to the roof to take a swim and a little dip in the hot tub?" he asked.

"You're on!"

Upstairs it was chilly, but the hot tub warmed us back up. I stayed there, not wanting to lose this cozy feeling, while Luke, as usual, jumped between the hot tub and the pool. Watching him made me smile as I remembered our first trip together as a couple.

We had been dating a month when Luke and I took our first trip to San Francisco.

"You ready for tomorrow?" he had asked as we admired the view of the sunset from our hotel room window the first night. "I have a day of nonstop action planned. First, we'll get a pass for the trolley so we can get anywhere in the city. Then we'll go to the trolley museum, the waterfront, and a few other stops I've highlighted." He'd tossed an earmarked travel magazine into my lap. "Then, in the evening, we'll hit up the pool for a swim and hot tub."

"I'm not much of a swimmer," I had confessed.

"No worries, I got you! Let's give it a go now!" Luke had jumped up and gotten into his suit. "Come on!" His childlike enthusiasm had been contagious.

I'd pulled on my swimsuit, grabbed a few towels, and followed him to the pool. He dove straight in, popping back up halfway across the pool. "It's nice in here. Come on in!" I'd dipped my toes in and cringed at the cold water. Luke did handstands, flips, and splashed about like a dolphin in play. I slowly lowered myself down the stairs with a bit of a shiver.

Luke swam over and grabbed me, kissing my face. He spun me around and tossed me in the air. I landed in the water. Now soaking wet, I splashed him. He splashed me back. We'd played that way for a long time, laughing the whole time. Luke grabbed me one more time and kissed me. "You know, Mags, I could get used to this. You best be careful." He kissed my face again.

My heart had swelled with love. I looked into his eyes. "Me too." I paused. "But now I'm cold. Hot tub?"

"Of course, my lady." He lifted me out of the pool and carried me to the hot tub. He gently set me down on the stairs, and I'd crawled in, dipping myself up to my neck. He sat next to me. "Better?" I smiled.

Not five minutes later, Luke had jumped back into the pool with a tremendous splash. He swam around for a few minutes, then joined me back in the hot tub. He repeated this action while I put my back against a jet and watched this wonderful man enjoy the evening. It had been perfect.

Now, at the Four Seasons, I could see that person again. He was having a blast and watching him brought me such joy.

Suddenly, he got out of the pool and clenched his stomach. "I need a bathroom." He ran to the men's room.

I followed and knocked on the door. "You okay, honey?" No response. "Honey?" We were alone, so I burst into the bathroom. Luke was passed out on the floor. I patted his face, and his eyes opened.

"I don't feel good."

"I've got you, honey." I rushed out and grabbed a towel and my cell phone. Back in the bathroom, I wrapped him up and called the front desk for help.

The bellboy came immediately, pushing a wheelchair. "He okay?"

Luke lay on the floor with his eyes closed. I grumbled at the stupid question. "Not really. Can we just get Luke back to the presidential suite?"

"No problem, ma'am," he said. I grabbed Luke under one armpit, and the bellboy grabbed the other. Together we lifted him into the chair. He moaned in pain but kept his eyes closed.

Back in our room, I tipped the bellboy and told him I'd leave the wheelchair out in the hall. Once he was gone, I stripped Luke's wet swimsuit off, dried him, and wrapped him up in bed. I lay down next to him and held him.

"I'm going to be sick," Luke said, waking me up. He tried to get out of the bed but fell to the floor. I handed him the ice bucket. He shook his head no. I put a plastic bag inside of it. He had no choice. He vomited repeatedly. I sat down next to him, rubbing his back.

When he was finished, I helped him into the bathroom, where he washed out his mouth and splashed his face with cold water.

"You want to go home, honey?"

"Nah, it was probably a bad oyster. I'll be fine." As I followed him back to bed, I realized I was still in my swimsuit. I changed into my floral pajamas. I removed the plastic bag from the ice bucket, tying it off with the expert touch of a woman who ties dog bags all the time.

A new bag in the ice bucket, I curled into bed next to him.

At two o'clock in the morning, I woke to the sound of Luke heaving. I came into the luxurious bathroom to find him on the floor, his skin greenish and his eyes sunken.

"What do you need?"

"Nothing a good sleep and some heated tile floors won't solve. But, hey, can you check my bag and see if I have my anti-nausea tablets?"

Relieved to find them, I passed some over.

"Go back to bed, love. I'll be there in a minute." I stood there, staring at him again, not knowing what he wanted. "Seriously, I said go. I'm not prepared to receive visitors right now," he said, trying to joke.

"Okay." I hesitantly headed back to the king-size bed and fell asleep.

Just after four in the morning, Luke was still on the floor where I'd left him, sound asleep. He looked so ill. We needed to go home. How did we get here again? I lay on the bed watching TV, keeping one eye on the bathroom doorway to see if Luke had woken up yet. I felt so lost, not knowing what to do. Finally, I crept into the bathroom. His eyes cracked open, just enough that I knew he could see me.

His whisper cut the silence. "I want to go home."

Less than an hour later, I parked the car at home and circled to help Luke out. Instead, he pushed my hands away. He staggered up the walkway. Staring at the five stairs leading to the porch, he raised a foot, then stopped with a look of defeat. I rushed over, reaching out for him. The leaves on the ground whooshed and woke up Westy, who began to bark inside.

Luke hesitantly grabbed my arm and began moving faster. Although he was a little green and slow-moving, I could see that Westy made him laugh as she pressed her dinosaur toy to the window by the door.

28

LOSING MY LUKE WAS TOP OF MIND, so I sat watching his chest rise and fall with growing snores. Was this our next step in this journey? Was he going to be ill for a long time?

At nine o'clock in the morning, I awoke to Westy licking my face.

"I know, girl, it's past breakfast time!" I put dry kibble into her bowl on the counter and added some hot water and a few cookie pieces. She danced around my feet, drooling. "Sorry, you have to wait!"

I set a timer for five minutes and went back into the bedroom. Luke was still asleep as I ran my hand over his bald head. His skin was greenish gray. My stomach clenched. I realized we still had a long way to go. We just no longer had to be at the hospital.

"Hi." Luke smiled weakly at me.

"Want tea or water or anything?"

"Water, please."

I filled the glass in the kitchen just as the timer went off. I put Westy's meal down and took the water into the bedroom.

"I'm so sorry I ruined our evening," Luke said. "I didn't mean to."

I leaned over and kissed his face. "Think we should call Oncology and see what is going on?"

"No, probably a bad oyster," he said again. I frowned. "I'm fine, Mags, really. I'm sure I'll be good as new by later today."

That night, while I was watching an episode of *Dateline*, I heard a *boom*, followed by quick, stumbling footsteps. I found Luke back at the toilet, getting sick. Westy curled up behind him.

"Honey, I really should call the oncology line."

"No! I'm fine, Mags." He threw up some more. I stayed there until he thought he was done and helped him back into bed. I wiped his face with a cold cloth, then refreshed his water. By the time I did that, he was back asleep.

I snuck upstairs into my office and called the oncology line. I told them what had happened over the past twenty hours.

"This is not unusual. It's probably the chemotherapy. The final treatment can be hard on the body. Take Luke's temperature and if he gets over 101 degrees, bring him back to the hospital."

I hung up the phone. When I came down the stairs, I heard Luke call me from the bedroom.

"Did you just sneak off and call Oncology?"

"Yes."

"I asked you not to."

"You are not the only person in this situation, Luke. I needed to know what I could do, so I called for me, not you."

"Whatever." He lay back down and went to sleep.

I had hoped we'd finished the sick days, sleeping and staying away from our lives.

THE FOLLOWING DAY, Ronnie appeared at our house.

"Is he done throwing up? That was gross."

"Really, the first thing out of your mouth is that?" I paused; she tapped her foot. "I'm not sure, but I think he might be," I said. "He slept through the night."

"Well, that's good." Ronnie pulled a bottle of champagne and orange juice out of her oversized purse. "I thought we could do a girls' morning and have mimosas."

"Sounds good to me." I smiled. "I'll just shut Luke's door so that he can sleep. Let's sit in the kitchen."

Ronnie and I poured a few mimosas and caught up. Ronnie updated me on the kitchen project, and I shared a few tidbits about projects I was working on and the blue sweater with a fox face on it that I was bidding on on eBay. It had been a few years since the conversation had flowed so effortlessly. I loved it.

"By the way, thanks for the Four Seasons room, Ronnie. It was amazing."

"I know, right? Devan has no idea what he missed. It was good for you." She paused. "Well, kinda."

"We got a few good hours in. Delicious food and drinks, and some playtime at the pool."

"Well, great!" she said. "I did hear from Devan last night. He apologized. He said he had met someone and didn't want to hurt me by telling me the truth." She exhaled heavily. "Like some twiggy girl is going to be better than me. He'll come to his senses."

I took another drink of my third mimosa. "But would you want him back even if he came begging?"

"I don't know." She flipped her shiny dark hair over her shoulder. "But I want to see him beg." She giggled. "Hey, I see there is a fundraising 5K for cancer patients tomorrow at Green Lake. Want to go with me?"

"Sure!" I declared. "What am I going to do here? Watch Luke sleep?"

"I guess we made them sorta strong," I slurred a little while later when we reached the bottom of two bottles of champagne and one orange juice.

"Mmm . . . hmm," Ronnie agreed. She walked into the living room and lay down on the carpet next to Westy. I finished up my drink and joined her.

It was dark outside when Luke tapped us both on the shoulder. "Hello, ladies. What are you doing? You smell like the end of a wedding celebration. Were you drinking already? It's only six."

We both started to giggle. "Yes," I said. "Ronnie brought stuff for mimosas, and I had to help her. How are you feeling?"

"Fine," Luke grumbled, then shook his head and walked into the kitchen.

"Tomorrow, we're going to do a 5K walk to raise money for cancer research," Ronnie stated proudly.

"I'm not a cancer survivor or a cancer patient. I'm just Luke." He glared at us from the doorway.

"Whatever, cranky pants. We're going to raise some cash for other 'noncancer' patients who happen to have cancer. Okay?"

I couldn't help but laugh.

"Wanna go outside, Westy?" Luke called out. Westy ran to the door, and they both left.

RONNIE AND I dressed in our walking gear at seven the next morning, ready to start the Kick Cancer 5K. We both had hangovers, but it felt good to be outside and doing something healthy for myself. As we walked, I forgot all the past few months' stress and enjoyed the fresh air and my sister's company.

We finished the race in forty minutes, which was slow but good enough. As we dropped off our tags that tracked when we'd started and finished, Ronnie caught the attention of an attractive much older man. He walked over to her.

"Well, hello! Are you a cancer survivor or a loved one?"

She gave him her million-dollar smile. "A loved one."

"Your husband is a lucky man."

"My brother-in-law. He's married to her." She pointed at me.

"I see. By chance, are you free for dinner tonight?" Ronnie tipped her head, about to decline, but he continued. "I'm the executive director of this nonprofit. I'm looking for a spokesperson and thought maybe you would be interested."

"I'd love to!" she said. "What time?"

"Want to meet at the Columbia Center restaurant at seven?"

"Sure," she said casually. "I'll see you there."

He walked away with a massive grin on his face.

"You tease," I said. "Why are you going?"

"To help people with cancer, of course. Why else?"

When I got home, Luke was watching TV. "How'd it go?" he asked coolly.

"Good. You still upset?"

"A little. I'm sick of the drunk routine."

"Routine?" I asked. "It's happened twice, honey. Twice."

"Twice while I'm sick, Mags. What if I had needed a ride to the hospital or help?"

"I'd call an ambulance?"

"Seriously," he spat, getting more frustrated by the minute.

"I'm sorry. You're right. I just got scared that you were so sick. I'm afraid the cancer is still there or even growing! So I let loose and kicked way too much alcohol back."

"I get it, but please try to not drink so much when I'm that sick. Okay, love?"

"I understand."

He asked me more questions about the walk. I told him about the older guy who had asked Ronnie out for dinner.

"Columbia Center? Cool, I want to go to that fancy place. Remember I pointed it out from the hospital?"

I nodded.

"Figures she gets to go first." Luke pouted.

"And she's talking about trying to get Devan's attention, god knows how she'll do that."

"Good god, woman, let it go!" he said as if Ronnie were in the room.

29

"I'D LIKE TO GO OUTSIDE and trim the smoke bush today," Luke said as we lay in bed that Sunday morning. "It looks super overgrown. I know spring is a way out, but it would be good to get that done and put the branches in the yard waste."

"Sounds good to me. You need my help?" I asked. "My plan for today is to make a big batch of Southwest chicken chili. I love having that for lunch on workdays. I'm back at work full-time starting tomorrow."

He smiled and kissed me on the cheek. "Good. Westy and I will do fine here. You just go and get your job back on track."

Opening all the cans for the chili is my least favorite part, but this simple dish is so good. Black, pinto, garbanzo, and navy beans go into the slow cooker, then one can of corn, a jar of my favorite salsa, two raw chicken breasts, water, and two teaspoons of chicken Better Than Bouillon. I let it cook for twelve or more hours and it makes enough to feed me lunch for a week or two. Thankfully I never get sick of it.

As I was putting the finishing touches on the batch, I heard a crash. Westy started to bark in the backyard. I ran. Luke and the ladder lay on the ground about five feet from the smoke bush.

"Are you okay?"

He sat up and shook his head. "The ladder is too heavy. I can't do it, Mags. I'm useless." He sat in the yard sobbing. I sat down next to him and held him. Westy stood over us, guarding us against an imaginary threat.

Luke sat on the couch for the rest of the day, watching action movies. He didn't speak. He didn't move. He didn't even pet Westy, who sat quietly at his feet, not moving an inch. I fussed about cleaning up in the kitchen until I ran out of things to do. I decided to go on a massive grocery shopping trip for everything I needed to make a bunch of freezer meals.

I filled a whole grocery cart with chicken breasts, flank steaks, all kinds of veggies, and staples at the store. Then, instead of leaving, I sat in the Safeway parking lot, staring at my phone. I hadn't done one of these large grocery runs since Luke got sick.

Usually, when I do one of these fill-up-my-car-all-the-way runs, I would text him that I was on my way home with a load of groceries when I finished my shopping. He would help me carry all the groceries into the house, working through the obstacle that is our dog. Then he would dig through the bags looking for the one with his prize: Snickers, Swedish Fish, and gummy Coke bottles. When Luke found it, he'd cheer and rip the bag open. Then he'd stack a Swedish Fish atop a gummy Coke bottle and take a bite. "Delicious!" he'd declare before making another treat. Then he'd stand in the kitchen and chat with me while I unloaded and sorted the groceries. He'd set up the freezer bag holders in sets of three, and I'd parse out the groceries into meals that we could pull out of the freezer in the morning and drop in the slow cooker, so by the end of the day, we'd have nothing to do but eat. I'd make red pepper chicken, spicy chicken with veggies, chili, and fajita bowls. The frozen meals made life easy and gave us time together.

But today felt different. I stared at the phone for a long time, trying to decide what would upset Luke least. Should I not text him, knowing he was weak and sore, and just march the groceries in on my own, or should I text him and risk him trying and failing again? The bag with the gummies and Snickers bar sat there, taunting me.

I began to cry. Once I started, I couldn't stop. The tears became sobs. It was hard to breathe. I put my face into my hands and leaned into my steering wheel. My life, our life, the life we had built, was gone. Finally, I sat up and began pounding on the steering wheel. I wanted to scream. I heard a door shut, and I turned to find an older woman looking in my window, her head tipped to the side. I knew she was silently asking me if I was okay. I wiped my face and forced a smile. She shared a sympathetic smile and then joined her husband as they walked into the store.

I watched this elderly couple and wondered if that would some-day be Luke and me. Would he be here when we were in our eighties? Would he be here in our fifties, for that matter? Would he gain his strength back? I took a deep breath, looking to regain control. I wiped my face, turned on the ignition, and backed out of my parking spot.

Ten minutes later, I pulled up in front of our house. I sat in the car, looking at my phone again. I decided to not text Luke this time. He was already so upset from the incident this morning that I couldn't bear causing more pain. Doing this cooking run had proba-bly been a bad idea, but there I sat with a load of perishable groceries in the back of the car. It was too late now.

Inside, I could see the points of Westy's ears as she watched every step I made. I grabbed a few bags and walked through the front door and past the white couch, where Luke sat. He looked up at me and shook his head.

"I'm too weak and useless to help with groceries now too?"

I put down the bags. "Love, I thought you needed some rest after your fall this morning."

He looked down at Westy. "Yup, useless. Fuck that, Mags."

I didn't want to fight. Maybe if I took out Luke's treats, he'd be happy. "I did get you these!" I said, tossing him two bags of gummies.

He caught them and immediately put them on the coffee table. "Gee, thanks."

"If you want to help, then help," I said, exhausted by this behavior.

"No, I'm good. Thanks." He lay down on the couch and stared at the TV.

I took four or five trips to and from the car, passing him with each load of groceries. Every time, he'd let out a huge sigh. I understood he was feeling bad, but what could I do?

When I was done, I shut and locked the front door, put the keys in the dish, and headed into the kitchen.

"Not gonna lock your car?"

"Guess not," I said, tired of this harassment. Luke stomped over to the key fob in the dish. *Beep beep.* He tossed the keys back into the dish with a clang and went back to his station on the couch.

I put my noise-canceling AirPods in my ears, turned on the audiobook *Brave New World,* and went about my work in the kitchen.

After an hour, I had about fifteen meals made and two more sets of three to go. I was happily listening to my book when I caught a glimpse of Luke in my periphery. I pulled my AirPods out of my ears.

"Goddamn it, Maggie. I've been trying to talk to you for five minutes, but you're tuned out. I thought I could help some in here."

"Oh, great!" I stated, trying to ignore his terse tone. "Wanna set up the next batch of bags? I'm going to get the red pepper chicken going."

"Sure." Luke grabbed three freezer bags and set them up with holders that keep them open. I got a cutting board out, and Luke began chopping onions and peppers while I cleaned the chicken and put the breasts in the bags.

"Shit!" Luke yelled, holding up his finger that was gushing blood.

"How deep is it?" I asked, pressing a paper towel on it. I pulled it back and saw it was a good cut but not one that would need stitches.

"Fuck."

"Luke, it's okay. Let's wrap it up. If you want to sit down and rest while the bleeding stops, I can keep going. It looks like the chopping is almost finished."

"No," he said, pushing past me. "I got this."

When Luke finished, he took the cutting board over to the bags and poured the peppers and onions on top of the raw chicken. He measured the seasonings and put them in a bowl, mixing them by hand. Then he grabbed a handful and dropped some of the mixtures in a bag. His sleeve caught the edge of the marination bag, crashing it onto the floor. Raw chicken, peppers, and onions were spread out everywhere. Westy jumped to her feet and came running into the kitchen.

"Leave it!" we both yelled in unison.

"Goddamn motherfucker." Luke threw the other two bags on the floor. He stormed out of the room, grabbed a coat, and slammed the front door on his way outside.

After cleaning up the floor with shaking hands, I finished the rest of the meals and sat down on the couch. But I was so mad that I couldn't sit still. I was furious that Luke had thrown the bags on the floor after making a mistake. I got that he was frustrated. But so was I. I decided to do some laundry to occupy my mind. Just as I pushed the button, I heard the front door close. My stomach was in knots. My hands started to shake again in anticipation of another argument. I walked into the living room, only to find it was Ronnie, not Luke, standing there with a bottle of wine.

"Hello, sissy!" she said, her smile fading. "What the hell is wrong with you? You look like someone pissed on your fireworks."

"Gross, Ronnie," I said, walking over to her for a hug. "Hello. What's going on? You look like you're up to something."

"Where the hell is Luke? I want to tell you both," she said, putting the wine in the fridge.

"He's out for a walk."

"Well, let's wait for him." Ronnie turned to Westy. "Wanna go play ball?" She grabbed one of Westy's balls from her toy bucket and walked to the back door. "Go get it, girl. Go, go, go!" she said as she threw the ball out into the yard.

Westy charged, catching the ball in her mouth. On her way back to us, she veered to the left. The ball came flying out from behind the smoke bush.

"Luke? You back there?" I called.

"Yep."

"Ronnie's here."

"I heard that."

"I've got news, Lukie. Come on in. It's exciting. You're going to love it. AND I brought wine!"

"Great," Luke grumbled, slowly coming out from behind the bush. Westy pushed her ball into his leg, asking for another throw. He obliged and then continued up the stairs, squeezing Ronnie as he passed her.

"Wanna open the wine for us?" Ronnie asked.

"Nope. You do it. I just break things," he said, leaving the kitchen.

"That's a shitty attitude, my friend."

"Whatever, Ronnie."

"I got it," I said.

Ronnie leaned over and whispered to me, "What's wrong with him?"

"Tough morning. Just let it go, okay?" I said. "Hey, how was your dinner with the older guy?"

"I'm here to tell you all about it!"

I opened the wine and poured two glasses. I grabbed a third and hesitated. "Luke, you want wine?"

"Yes, please."

"At least you still have some manners," Ronnie yelled. I kicked her ankle.

"Leave it. Seriously, Ronnie, leave him alone."

Ronnie grabbed her wine, and I brought a glass out for Luke. I sat next to him on the couch. He slid away from me.

"Luke, I don't know if Mags told you, but the executive director of the Kick Cancer nonprofit invited me to dinner at Columbia Center, and it was glorious. Did you know they have windows in the women's bathroom, so you can look out over the city from the eightieth floor or something wild like that?"

"Wow," I said. "You in love with this guy now?"

She rolled her eyes. "Anyway, that's not the cool part." She stood up and twirled. "He asked me to be the spokesperson for their charity!"

"What exactly does that mean?" Luke asked flatly.

"I'm so glad you asked! I get to go to their events around the state and talk about my experience having a loved one with cancer. Then I do the big asks to raise money for people like you guys. How amazing is that? I don't even have to quit my job since most of this happens on weekends."

Luke's face began to turn red. "Are you fucking serious, Ronnie? No, I say no. You do not own my story. You are not a part of my story. I will never forgive you if you use my cancer to get attention. Why the hell are you doing this?"

Ronnie fell backward into the chair. "I . . . I . . . I'm surprised you don't want me to help people going through cancer."

"No, Ronnie, I don't. You aren't helping. You're a pain in the ass. Do not take this job. If you do, I will never forgive you. EVER." He stormed out of the room and back into the yard. Westy picked up her ball and followed behind.

Ronnie stared at me, red rims highlighting her eyes. "I just wanted to help."

I tipped my head, willing her to tell the truth. She just stared at me. "And?"

"Okay, so I wanted Devan to see me doing something good. Maybe then he'd come back. But it's a win-win."

"Luke is private, Ronnie. If you drag Luke into this, it will not go well."

"Well, fuck that, and fuck you guys. I'm going to do this." She stood to leave, then paused at the door, as if waiting for me to follow her like I usually did. I did not follow. I did not try to make it up to her.

"Ronnie, do not do this. Please. For me? For Luke?"

Ronnie walked out the door, slamming it behind her.

I plopped back down on the couch and finished my wine, as well as Luke's leftovers.

30

FOR THE FIRST TIME IN MONTHS, my alarm went off at seven the next morning. After a shower and breakfast, I used my phone flashlight to navigate the dark bedroom and put together my outfit: a cute top, cardigan, and some nice jeans. Leaning over Luke, I kissed his face.

"I'm off to work, honey."

"Okay," he said groggily.

"You want some coffee before I go?"

"Nope." He rolled over in bed, his back to me.

At work, I sat down at the desk I had abandoned back in September.

My assistant, Etta, came bounding in, running over to hug me. "Oh my god! You're back, and Luke is good."

I smiled. I had missed her positive attitude and shine. "I'm back! Now let's get this train going!"

Etta caught me up on the most recent developments. "There are a ton of events that we should go to, like the Bellevue Chamber, Seattle Chamber, and a few dinners with the Amazon people. Shall I start lining them up?"

"Yes, but I want to be home for dinner with Luke most nights. If we can do happy hours or lunch meetings, that would be best."

"You got it," she said, sitting back down at her computer to begin getting things organized.

Colleagues stopped by and asked how Luke was doing. A few told me about production nightmares that had happened while I was away. It felt great to be back at work. A sigh of relief escaped me. This felt normal. I wasn't the cancer patient's wife here. I wasn't someone to take out his anger on. I was a member of the business team. I had a job to do, and I was good at it. The darkness of the past few months began to fade as a brighter outlook started to appear.

Netflix was playing back-to-back episodes of *Top Gear*, Luke's favorite car show, when I got home that night. I could hear him snoring as I made a pork loin dinner with roasted Brussels sprouts and rice.

I shook Luke's shoulder. "Dinner is ready. I set the table." I kissed his face.

"No, thanks," he said, going back to sleep.

I plated my dinner and sat at the table, listening to *Brave New World*. It was delicious, but that didn't cheer me up. I hated eating dinner alone.

Afterward, I put a few meat scraps in Westy's bowl, then wrapped up a plate of food for Luke. His eyes were open when I joined him in the living room.

"Did Westy get dinner?" I asked.

"Nope."

"Okay, I'll do that now. I also made up a plate for you to reheat when you get hungry."

"Okay."

"How was your day?"

"Fine."

I left him there, watching TV, and went to feed Westy. I watched as she plowed through her dinner without chewing. When she finished licking her bowl, she came over and nuzzled me. I squatted down next to her. "Wanna take a walk, girl?"

Westy began grumbling and barking with excitement.

"I'm going to take Westy for a walk. Want to come?"

"Nope."

The cold air on my face felt good. We walked for an hour. When I got back, Luke was in bed, sound asleep. I sat in the front window, drinking chamomile tea, my feet warmed by Westy. Couples walked by, all bundled up. Some held hands. Some walked their dogs. Many were chatting and laughing, taking in the evening after a day at work. I remembered when Luke and I would walk Westy at the end of the day. I longed for that time and connection. Instead, my marriage felt closer to the relationship one would have with a neighbor. It dawned on me that when he was going through treatment, we'd had a common enemy. Now we were dropped back into our lives that in no way resembled what we had before cancer, and we didn't know how to relate. But what would I do about that?

The rest of the week was more of the same. I stopped putting meals together for Luke since he didn't seem to eat them.

When Saturday came, I hoped that Luke would be more open to hanging out. He wasn't. Mostly, he just stared blankly at the TV.

Monday morning, I arrived at work early.

"I'm still not used to you being back. It's so great!" Etta said when she arrived.

"It's good to be back."

"How was your weekend? How is Luke?"

"Luke is doing good. My weekend was fine. How was yours?"

"Andrew and I took a drive up to Leavenworth and walked around in the shops. It was a lot of fun. Well, until he threw a snowball at me. Then he was up for a fight. It was a blast!"

"Sounds fun." I smiled at her, but my heart hurt. I missed my partner, my love, my playmate. "This week, I'd love to get some client dinners in. Can you schedule a few?"

31

TIME FLEW BY. I got up every morning, fed Westy, kissed Luke goodbye, and went to work. At the end of my workday, I'd attend a dinner meeting and get home around eight at night. Luke was usually passed out on the couch when I got home. I'd kiss him hello. We'd watch an episode of *Schitt's Creek* or *Billions*, then go to bed. On the weekends, I'd walk Westy, meet some friends for a meal or drinks, and read. It was hard to remember that we'd had so much hope when he finished treatment.

Rinse and repeat for two weeks.

Until my phone rang in the middle of a dinner with a potential client.

"Where are you?" Luke asked.

"At Serafina with the group from Zillow. Why?"

"Please come home."

"Is everything okay?" My stomach curled up in knots. Luke had been feeling ill and sleeping most of the time. Was cancer growing again?

"I'm okay, but I need you."

"I'll wrap this up and be home as soon as I can. You're sure you're okay?"

"Physically, yes."

Westy and Luke were sitting at the front window when I got home, watching me get out of my car. I rushed up the path.

Westy danced around my feet as Luke, behind her, reached out for a cuddle. It had been weeks since we had been close. I could hear him start to cry. I held him tighter, beginning to sob myself.

We stood there for a long time, holding one another, not speaking. Finally, Westy pushed her way between us, and we both began to belly laugh.

"What's going on, honey?" I asked as I hung up my coat and Luke started pacing.

"You want tea, wine, or anything?" he said as if I hadn't spoken.

"No, I'm fine," I said in a calm voice, hoping to slow him down.

"I can't take it anymore, Mags. I can't."

"What happened?"

"Your sister. Your sister is what happened." Luke relayed a scene that had played out two hours earlier.

Luke had been feeling terrible all day. His stomach was cramping; he felt hot and could barely keep his eyes open. Finally, he fell into a deep sleep.

He awoke to Westy barking at the door. Then he heard the lock and the door open. He figured it was me, but instead Ronnie appeared at his bedroom door.

Luke pretended to be asleep, hoping she'd go away. He didn't want to see her after their fight about her becoming a cancer spokesperson.

"Luke, you awake?" Ronnie whispered.

Silence.

"Luke?" A little louder this time. Still no answer.

"Luke? Where's Maggie?" When he didn't answer, she turned the light on. "Luke?"

"What the fuck do you want, Ronnie?"

"Is Mags home?"

"No, she's working late. Again. Get out of here, Ronnie. I don't feel good."

She paused in the doorway as if considering her options. Finally, she spoke. "Here's the deal. My new job as a spokesperson is about to start. And tonight the national news wants to do a story. Isn't that great?"

"No."

She ignored him. "Tonight, the story will run live. It will only be a five-minute piece. I need you to get dressed and come to the station to launch this interview. Think of all the money we can raise and the families we can help."

"Get out, Ronnie."

"No, it will take one hour. Get up, Luke. I'll take you to Columbia Center if you're good."

"Get the fuck out of my house, Ronnie," Luke demanded.

Ronnie walked over to the bed and pulled Luke's arm. He grabbed the headboard, trying to stay put, but was too weak to hold on. With one determined pull, Ronnie ripped him out of bed.

"Get up, Luke. We need to go."

"Fuck off."

"Now!" she yelled.

Luke got back into bed.

Ronnie ripped off all the covers.

Luke got up.

"That's more like it, Luke. You'll be so glad you did this." Ronnie twinkled, seeming pleased she had won this battle of wills.

Luke walked past her into the bathroom, Westy on his heels. He locked the door with a loud click, then pulled two towels off the rack and made a makeshift bed on the floor.

Ronnie began banging on the bathroom door. She yelled at him, calling him selfish and childish and even an asshole.

"Ronnie," he raged through the door, "you are a selfish, manipulative bitch. You are not welcome in my house ever again." He punched the door. When he caught his breath, he curled up in a ball on the floor, tears streaming down his face.

An hour later, he woke up with Westy licking his face. He cracked open the hard white door to find the coast clear. As he lay down in bed, his head hit a sheet of paper with a message scrawled in Ronnie's red lipstick.

SELFISH BASTARD! You are ruining my life!

His hands began to tremble as fury rose from his toes to the top of his head. All he wanted was his wife. He wanted me.

"Oh, honey, I'm so sorry." I held Luke as he cried.

"I'm mad. I'm sad. I'm frustrated. I feel useless." He sobbed. I rocked him back and forth on the couch until he fell asleep. Then I grabbed my keys and drove to Ronnie's apartment.

"What the fuck do you want?" Ronnie said as she swung the door open. "Your husband is single-handedly ruining my life."

"You have got to be kidding me. You're the asshole. You tried to drag a cancer patient out of bed after he told you he felt bad. Don't you get it? He's sick. He's a private person. He is not your pawn in a game to win back some guy. Some guy who clearly doesn't want you. What the hell is wrong with you?"

"You are so selfish, Maggie."

"Me?" I laughed in her face. "Me? You're the one torturing a man who has been through hell."

"He's fine. He beat cancer. Now you need to help others. Besides, you just baby him. You like the attention and don't want to share it with me."

"Oh my god. What is wrong with you?"

"All I'm trying to do is help cancer patients around the world, and your husband just swears at me and bans me from your house. Then you"—she began to yell louder and louder—"come over here and call me names? I'm the one who lost my job tonight, thanks to Luke. You guys owe me."

My jaw stiffened. I wanted to punch Ronnie so badly. But instead I just stood there, fuming, fists clenching.

"Go on, punch me. Do it." Ronnie glared. "Give me a reason to press charges."

I turned on my heel and walked back to my car. Ronnie was still standing in her doorway.

I lowered my window. "I never want to see you again!" I yelled before hitting the gas and squealing my way out of her neighborhood.

Luke was awake when I got home.

"Where did you go?"

"I confronted Ronnie. I'm with you. She is no longer allowed in this house."

"Time for bed?" he asked.

"Yes!"

For the first time in weeks, we curled up together and slept the night through.

The next morning, I woke up late and had to rush through my morning routine. By the time I got my shoes on, Luke was standing there with a to-go cup of coffee for me. I leaned in and kissed him, remembering the first time I'd spent the night years ago.

When we started dating, I was determined to take it slow, the pain of a recent breakup still fresh. After a first date at Salty's on Alki drinking wine, munching on coconut prawns, and laughing like children, Luke and I had planned a second date. I'd canceled it at the last minute because of a fight with Ronnie that had upset me almost as much as she had this time. One hour later, my phone had dinged as I sat at my desk typing away on my computer.

Luke: *Sorry about tonight. Call me if you need to talk. I'm here.*

My last boyfriend had not been interested in my sisterly issues. He'd tell me to save my complaints for my girlfriends. Then he'd leave the room. And here was this guy I'd had dinner with once and he was ready to talk? I was blown away. I didn't answer right away, but two days later, I was still thinking about him and how kind his message was. I texted him, and he invited me to his roommate's birthday.

I got tipsy that night and needed a sleepover. Even though I had insisted on sleeping in a different room, in the morning he brought me a cup of coffee with a big smile on his face and his dog, Belle. in tow. My heart melted, and I knew right then that he was a keeper.

"Hello. Earth to Maggie. You there?"

"Oh, yes! Just remembering the first time you brought me coffee. I love that you still deliver my morning hit of caffeine to this day!" I kissed his face. "Do you have time to feed Westy?" I asked.

"Got it. Both feeding Westy and making your coffee for life." He smiled, and his eyes had a bit of a twinkle—a sign my Luke was still in there.

WHEN I OPENED MY COMPUTER AT WORK, I was bombarded by a flurry of personal emails, each from a different friend angry at my sister, all including a link to my sister's YouTube page, expressing concern and asking me what the hell was going on.

I clicked on the link and couldn't believe my eyes. There was a recording of my sister wearing a sexy fitted black dress in her living room, talking about Luke and his cancer journey. I scrolled down, and there were about twenty clips, each between two and five minutes long. I turned up the audio.

"It's hard being a caregiver. My brother-in-law, Luke, needed constant attention. Attention my sister alone could not provide. I found it hard to drop my social life to help them, but I did. I was there when they needed me, which is what family is for. To be there for one another when the going gets tough. When my sister broke down, I was there with cocktails. When Luke had trouble sleeping, I tucked him into bed. Taking this much care and being selfless is what it means to be family. This is true love."

My hands began to tremble, my heart racing. I told Etta that I had an emergency that needed handling right away and left the office. I called Luke in my car.

"Honey, have you seen it?" I asked the moment he picked up the phone.

"Yes," he said, sounding defeated.

"Are you okay?"

"Yes, I'm fine. Ronnie's the one who looks like an idiot. I just wish she would stop. These lies on her YouTube page are over the top, even for her."

"I know. I'll deal with it."

"Thank you. Hey, are you going to be home tonight?"

"Um . . . I can be. Yes, yes, I will be home."

"See you then!"

"Love you."

"Ditto, ditto, beep." I smiled for a moment before remembering another call had to be made.

Ronnie didn't answer, so it was message time. "Goddamn it, Ronnie. You are such a liar. Take it all down." My hands trembled as I hung up. I sat in my car for a few more minutes. My heart was still racing.

Exiting the car, I paced the parking lot, willing my phone to ring. Nothing.

I called Ronnie again—no answer—then did it again five minutes later.

Time to stop obsessing. I cut my losses for now and went inside to Etta's desk.

"Can you cancel my dinner for tonight, please?"

"Everything okay?"

"It will be." I sighed. "It will be eventually."

That night, my cute little family greeted me at the door with kisses. As I put my things down, I noticed a candlelit dining room table all set.

I smiled. "What's this, Luke?"

"Please, take a seat." He pulled the chair out for me. "Tonight, madame, we have a wonderful dinner for you. I picked up your favorite from Joli, prime rib."

I laughed. "I wondered if we were having ham and cheese or macaroni and cheese."

"No, madame, not tonight. Tomorrow I will serve ham and cheese." He grinned. I smiled and stood to kiss his face.

As we were finishing up our excellent meal, I took a chance and broached a difficult subject. "I've noticed you've been down lately."

"Yeah, but I'm getting better."

"Yes, I can see that. But may I make a suggestion?"

"Sure."

"Maybe it's time that we both go into counseling. Separately and together. We have both been through so much. What do you think?"

"I'm okay. I'm doing better."

"You are, honey. You seem happier. But we need to rebuild our life."

"We do," Luke admitted. "It's felt weird since we got home this last time."

"I know. I've felt that too. I've been missing you. Missing us." I spun my wedding ring around my finger.

He watched, fidgeting with his ring. "Me too. Okay. We must find our way through the life we have now. I'll try it. Both types of counseling. That is, I'll go if you take over the cooking again."

I laughed. "You bet. I couldn't agree more."

AFTER DINNER, we had settled in to watch TV when there was a knock at the door, followed by Westy barking. I looked at Luke.

"That has to be Ronnie. What do you want to do?"

"Shake some sense into her?" he said with a wink. "She's still your sister."

"Shall I answer? I think I should."

"Then go for it."

I opened the door. Ronnie jumped into my arms and held me tight. "I'm so, so sorry, sissy. I'm so sorry."

I pushed her away. "I'm not ready for this."

"I understand. I did terrible things. Can I please talk to you? And if you want me to leave after that, I will. Promise."

"I'm listening." I crossed my arms.

"Can I come in and apologize to Luke too?"

"You're pushing it."

Luke stepped behind me and motioned her in.

She walked toward Luke with her arms out. He waved her away. Ronnie sat down on the footstool near his side.

"I'm such an asshole. I got so wrapped up in trying to win Devan back. I didn't listen to you. I posted those videos on YouTube to raise money for cancer patients' families and show both Devan and the nonprofit folks that I was worthy of them. Then a few cancer patient caregivers reached out, and I didn't know how to help them. One woman told me I was a phony and began to cry. That hurt. Then, I remembered your worn-out face and imagined how I was wasting the little energy you had to spare. I can't do that to people. Believe it or not, I'd hoped to help. At least that was part of it. I've taken the videos down now. I think I'm starting to realize how much I've made this all about me, and it's not. It's about you. It's about Luke. It's about people with loved ones fighting for their lives. I'm sorry." She began to cry.

I sat down next to Luke on the couch. Both of us were silent, in pure shock. It was rare to get an apology out of Ronnie.

Luke leaned forward. "It's okay. We all make mistakes. Just please do not do that again to me."

"Oh my god, no. I tried to pull you out of bed when you were sick. It's almost like I was possessed. I'm such a jerk. How can I make it up to you? How can I help?"

"I don't know that I'm buying this." I crossed my arms. "Why now? Why should we believe you." Luke looked shocked. I stared.

"I'm saying I'm sorry, sissy, I really am."

"Why now? Be honest."

Ronnie twisted on her seat. "Today, I went to another cancer fundraising walk and tried to offer my help. When I arrived at the check-in counter, I faced an angry crowd of about six caregivers. They called me a liar, a fake, a phony. I'm betting the leader was the one I mentioned before." She paused to rub her eyes. "Anyway, I told them I just wanted to help, and they wouldn't listen. They dumped a whole water cooler of fruit punch over my head, ruining my new white shoes. Then another one pushed me onto the ground. I looked for help in the crowd but no one helped. They just ignored me. I sat in my puddle of punch until a bald little girl who was probably only six came over and sat next to me. She asked me if I was hurt and wanted help. She handed me a stuffed toy elephant and said that when she went to the hospital her Dumbo helped her believe it was all going to be okay. She asked me to hold it and believe as she put her little arm around me. Her mother came over to us and looked at me for a moment and nodded with recognition. The little girl smiled as I handed her toy back. Before she left she told me, 'As long as you have family that love you, you can do anything.' And then she walked away holding her mother's hand. I realized you are the only family I have and I have treated you terribly."

My usual bulldog of a sister was sitting on a stool, slumped over in sorrow. My anger for her melted away, and compassion took over. I leaned in and kissed her head.

"Want some prime rib? We have leftovers from Joli."

32

LUKE WAS FEELING BETTER EVERY DAY, and his hair was even starting to grow back. But I kept shaving it because it was still clumpy on top of his head. As I got out the machine and he stepped into the bathtub, I noticed that his chest was hairy again too, but it looked different. The curls met in the middle and pushed out on each side as if there were a seam running down his chest.

"What've you got going on here?" I asked, pulling on a long chest hair.

"Looks to me like a faux chest-hawk," he said, laughing.

"Want to keep it?" The electric razor jumped to life. "Or do you want me to shave it off?"

"Shear me! Shear me, baby!"

I shaved his head with a short guide and moved it up one level for his chest. I hesitated around the port. I wished they had removed that reminder of chemotherapy, of hard times. Had they left it there because they thought cancer would come back? I shook off my fears as I finished shaving him. While Luke showered, I got ready for our appointment with our therapist.

Luke and I stepped into the familiar office where we'd had counseling years ago and still returned to occasionally for check-ins. Kim had helped us sort out problems in the past where there seemed to be no middle ground.

"What brings you in today?" Kim asked as we sat down in our usual chairs. We told her about the last five months of chemo and recovery.

"When is your next PET scan?"

"In two days," Luke said.

"Nervous?"

"Yes!" we both said in unison.

"I'll bet. How are you feeling, Luke?" He told her how he'd felt useless and depressed for a while but was coming out of it.

She turned to me. "How about you?"

"I'm fine."

Luke shook his head. "Sure, being a cancer patient was hard. But I feel like it was harder for you. My job was to follow directions. You kept trying to help, and there was little you could do other than be there."

"It WAS hard." I turned to Luke. "But not as scary as facing your mortality."

"You faced it too." He reached out for my hand, and I grabbed his.

"I was so scared I was going to lose you and be left alone. I don't want to be without my best friend. Remember all those deaths on the oncology floor? Becca's mom, the young family, Denise's friend?" I began to sob. "I don't know who I am without my Luke."

"I'm not going anywhere, Mags." He smiled.

"You two have been through a lot. It's going to take time to process everything that happened. All the fear. I'm glad to see you are both in individual counseling as well as coming here together. How are you feeling physically, Luke?"

"Pretty weak," he said matter-of-factly. "I hate it."

"That is normal. Your body has been through a lot. You should look into physical therapy."

"Why?"

"Your body has changed through the treatment. A physical therapist can help you build yourself back up without hurting yourself. I know you. You get going on a project and don't want to stop. You could hurt yourself."

"You could," I said.

"Maggie, what are you doing now?" Kim asked.

"I'm back at work. I love it. It feels so normal. But for a while there, I did notice I was avoiding home. I had my assistant schedule dinner meetings almost every night because it was hard to see Luke on the couch. I feel terrible about that."

"Yeah, I didn't like that at all. I knew what you were doing," Luke said. "But I wasn't exactly the nicest guy."

"So, what are you doing differently now?" Kim asked.

"We're having dinner together and talking more," I said. Luke and I smiled at one another.

"That's a good start. Remember what I always say?"

In unison, we repeated, "Do not compromise; negotiate."

"Right. What do you need, Luke?"

"Time to regain my old strength."

"Maggie, can you give him that time?"

I hesitated. "Yes. How much time?"

"I don't know. Can we take it one day at a time?" he asked.

"Maggie, what do you need?"

"I still need time with you. I want to take walks, go for a drive, and watch a movie. I just miss us being . . . well . . . us."

"Sounds fair. Luke?"

"I'd really like that."

I grabbed his hand and squeezed.

"Great, you two. Good work. See you next week? Your homework is, Luke, find yourself a physical therapist and spend more time with Maggie. Maggie, you support Luke by giving him time to heal."

THAT NIGHT, Ronnie showed up with two enormous bags of food and a man.

"Got some time for dinner and a chat?"

I stepped back and invited them to make themselves comfortable while I ran downstairs to Luke's workshop, where he was tinkering with a broken watch.

"Drake, this is my sister, Maggie, and my brother-in-law, Luke," Ronnie said once we were all assembled in the living room.

"Nice to meet you." Drake shook my hand and Luke's.

"I wanted you guys to meet. Since my little, shall we say, snafu, I have been looking for a way to show you how very sorry I am. I did some research and found out that Drake here is the best physical therapist in the area. I don't know if you were considering physiotherapy. But I thought if I could connect you guys, Luke could ask Drake some questions."

Luke looked over at me. I shook my head: no, I had not told Ronnie about Kim's suggestion.

"That's cool. I was just thinking of looking for a physical therapist. Tell me about what you do, Drake," Luke said.

Drake talked about how different cancers need different recovery protocols. For example, since chemo treatments often impact overall muscle mass and the heart and lungs, he worked with patients on conditioning the muscles first and then got them into cardio exercise.

"That sounds great! Let's sort out the details later and just enjoy our dinner now."

Ronnie pulled out Luke's favorite Chinese dishes, cashew chicken and General Tso's chicken, and mine, moo goo gai pan.

As we chatted about our plans for the rest of the winter, it felt like old times. Before cancer.

33

TWO DAYS LATER, it was time for Luke's PET scan. We decided we wanted to start the day together, walking Westy.

Holding her leash for the first time since he'd fallen, Luke walked with confidence. He pulled her back into a heel a few times before she gave up and stuck to his side. We rounded the corner, and all was going well. Then a cat came running off its porch and in front of us. I paused. Luke pulled back on Westy's leash and made her sit. She obeyed, staring at the cat, grumbling her barks.

"No bark, Westy. No bark," Luke said sternly.

Once the cat was out of sight, we continued the short loop. It was nice to be out, but Luke didn't want to overdo it. He had a physical therapy appointment with Drake in one week.

At the end of our walk, Luke let Westy off her leash. She ran back to the house and pushed on the crack of the door with her nose, whining.

"Yes, I'll get you a cookie, girl," Luke said with a chuckle. I rubbed his back while he unlocked the door.

ARRIVING AT SWEDISH still made my stomach churn.

Upstairs, we sat in the lobby while Luke drank his radioactive drink. An older man across from us was also drinking his.

"What flavor you got?" he asked.

"Berry. You?" Luke asked.

"Espresso. One thing is for sure—if you get the banana one, you burp banana all day. It's terrible. Never get banana."

"I'll keep that in mind," Luke said with a smile.

The older man was called in first. Then the nurse said Luke's name.

The nurse told me it would be about an hour, so I decided to take a trip back through the tunnels to the Starbucks on Madison. I wanted a coffee but didn't have the heart to get one from the hospital lobby. Those memories associated with chemo were still too fresh.

Outside the Starbucks, I saw Queenie.

"Would you like a coffee today, Queenie?"

"Yes, I'd like a—"

"Hazelnut latte with half-and-half?"

"Yes. One of those. I remember you," she said with a smile. "You're back. It's been a while."

"My husband is in for a PET scan today." She listened, her eyes wandering toward the front door of the Starbucks. "Right, I'll go get the coffee. Anything to eat?"

"An everything bagel with cream cheese?"

"You got it."

While I waited for my drinks, a businessman came in and ordered a soy latte. It was the guy who spilled my coffee all those months ago. What a jerk.

The barista called out my soy latte first, but the man went to grab it.

"I'm sorry, sir, this one is mine." I took a sip to lay claim to my coffee.

He looked at me with tired eyes and smiled. "Oh, sorry about that. I'm just distracted."

He seemed sad upon closer inspection. Had I been so caught up in my grief that I didn't stop to consider what he might be going through?

Soon after, the rest of my order was ready. I took everything outside and handed the bagel and drink to Queenie.

"Thank you," she said. "Oh, I need to go." She left me and ran across the street toward a woman with a shopping cart. I watched with a smile as they hugged and sat down in the other bus shelter.

An hour later, Luke returned to the waiting room.

"How'd it go?" I asked.

"Fine."

"When will we know?"

"Tomorrow afternoon."

I took a deep breath. "Great."

"I'm fine, I can tell. I'm doing great!"

"Then why aren't they taking out your port?"

He laughed. "Is that what's been bugging you? I noticed you hesitated over it when you were helping me shave."

"Busted," I admitted. "I just worry."

"A lot," he said. "An awful lot. I'm okay, Mags." He rested his arm across my shoulders as we walked out together.

THE NEXT DAY, I worked from home so I'd be there for the PET scan call. I knew Luke was confident, but I wasn't. I was returning emails when I heard Luke come through the front door, back from running errands. I ran downstairs.

"Any news?" I said.

"Yeah! I've got epic news!"

"And?" I said, my heart stopping while he paused.

"I'm the proud father of three broken antique clocks. I went to this antiques shop to find a new band for this watch, and I saw these. The guy made me a killer deal. I'm planning to fix them. Want to see?"

I let out the breath I'd been holding. "Sure. But did the hospital call you with the results?"

"Nope, not yet."

"Isn't it bugging you?"

"Nope. Let's go look at the clocks."

"Okay." Luke grabbed my hand and pulled me outside to the car. "How do you stay this calm?" I asked.

"It's not like sitting around worrying is going to change anything. And look how cool these are."

Luke showed me three clocks, all from the late nineteenth century. One was black marble, one was a grand-looking German clock, and one was shaped like a pope's hat.

"Wow, this is beautiful!" I said, picking one up. "How are you going to fix these? What do you know about clocks?"

"Clocks, engines. It's all the same. The parts are just smaller." He grinned.

"You're amazing!" I smiled and kissed his cheek. We carried the clocks inside, and Luke picked the marble one to take downstairs to his workshop.

I went back upstairs, my ears perked for a ringing phone.

Around four o'clock, I heard something. I flew down my stairs and met Luke coming up from the basement. "I'm clear!" he yelled.

I squealed. "You did it, love. You did it!"

"We did it!" Luke said, kissing my face. "I've been thinking about something else."

"Oh, do tell."

"How about holding off on a trip to Hawaii, maybe go with my folks when my dad gets better? They love it there and it would be something for him to look forward to. Does that sound good?"

"Sure," I said, watching my dreams of a post-cancer trip fade into the sunset.

"But what are these?" he said, handing me a manila envelope.

I opened the cream envelope to find stark white plane tickets to Copenhagen. "What?!?! You are up for Europe?" I began to jump up and down, overcome with excitement. Was Healthy Luke finally leaving the country? Going to one of my favorite places on the planet?!

"Yes, ma'am. I bought those anticipating the death of Arnie and voila, here we are. Ronnie even said she'd take—"

I squealed so loud I didn't hear the rest of his sentence. Westy came bounding into the room, a tennis ball clenched in her jaw getting squeezed until it squeaked too.

"Thank you, thank you, thank you!"

"Thank YOU for being there for me."

I grabbed him into an embrace. "I have so much planning to do!" With that, I was off to my computer to start my research.

34

WINTER TURNED INTO SPRING. The flowers coming up in our yard released a sweet fragrance. Luke and I left the house, walking down the path to the car. Today was the big day. Luke was having his six-month checkup, and they would remove his port.

While Luke went into the back, I sat in the all-too-familiar waiting room. I saw a few people drinking the radioactive drinks, sitting next to worried-looking loved ones. Others sat alone in a mask, staring blankly at the front desk. My heart went out to each of the people on their cancer journey. No two journeys are the same, but each is hard in its own way. I was hopeful that today we would get another all-clear. But I also realized that my life had changed in an instant before, and nothing could stop that from happening again.

My phone buzzed, drawing my attention. It was an email from Jenn at Spark.

Maggie,

We are considering your idea for *Maven* for the fall. Can you and your team come in and discuss logistics? It would be great to get this project going.

Thank you,
Jenn

I nearly squealed with joy as I forwarded the incredible message to my team with a quick note: We're in!

A few minutes later, Luke came out beaming. "I'm all clear, honey! And I'm port-free!" I grabbed him. "Careful there. It's pretty sore."

"Oh, sorry, love." I kissed his face. "I also have good news!"

"Better than mine? Tell me now, woman!"

"Spark called, and they want us to come in and discuss details about *Maven*! Finally, my branded show may become a reality!" I jumped up in the air.

"I'm so proud of you! I can't wait to celebrate."

Ronnie had promised a special night out to celebrate the cancer all-clear and my pitch moving forward. She showed up at six o'clock on the dot. But, instead of getting out of the car, Ronnie sat in the street, honking. Luke and I rushed out to meet her before she disturbed the whole neighborhood.

"Geez, Ronnie, honking? Really?" I asked, sliding into the back seat. Luke walked around to the front and noticed a man was already there. It was Drake.

"Oh, hi!" Luke said with a grin. "I wondered."

"Drake was telling me how well you were doing, so I thought he should join us for the celebration. I hope you don't mind."

"Not at all!" I looked at Luke and smiled. Drake was so much nicer than Ronnie's usual choices. If he could handle her brand of crazy, then she was all his.

Twenty minutes later, we pulled up in front of the Columbia Center.

"Get out," Ronnie said. "Just go up to the seventy-fifth floor and say you are here with Ronnie."

"You got a reservation? How cool is that?" Luke and I jumped out of the car and rushed in.

When Ronnie and Drake arrived, they joined us at a unique round table in the dining room. We could see Swedish Hospital sitting atop the hill. I thought of all the times I had looked out those lit-up windows at this exact spot, dreaming of the day when our lives would go back to normal. Now I knew our lives would never be quite the same, but we had learned something valuable through all the pain. We'd learned to appreciate life. We had known it was fleeting before our journey with cancer started, but now both Luke and I felt it in every cell of our body. Life was good.

ABOUT THE AUTHOR

Photo credit: Scott Finley, Mighty Media Studios

Maren is an Emmy-nominated producer and writer. Some of her favorite career highlights include working on *Deadliest Catch*, *Oprah's Big Give*, and *Jockeys*. After many years in the industry, she decided to update her skills and received her master's in digital communications from the University of Washington in June of 2015.

At the beginning of her career, Maren's desire to work in production and film took her to Ithaca College's film school and an internship at an advertising agency in London, England. Upon graduation, she immediately moved to LA following her dream of writing and directing films.

After a few years of working on a variety of projects, in 2001 she found herself entrenched in the brand-new reality TV business. Maren's passion for telling others' true-to-life stories inspired her to write a fictional novel as a reflection of actual occurrences in her life as a single, successful professional. Her novel, *Lana Fray and the Grand Plan*, became the 2015 IndieReader Discovery Award winner for the chick-lit category.

Maren decided to slow her life down and move back to her hometown, Seattle, Washington, where she met her beloved husband. Less than five years into their marriage, Maren's husband, Brandon, was diagnosed with inoperable lymphoma. To assume the role of caregiver, Maren stepped down from her roles on a talk show called *Modern Workplace*. Her employer, Mighty Media Studios, created a role for her to run business development, which she could do from the hospital room while her husband was doing five-day, twenty-four-hour-a-day in-hospital chemotherapy, which took place six times.

This pushed Brandon and Maren into the world of cancer full time. They worked through the process together and used humor to battle the fear.

Today, Brandon has been in remission for five years. To help others that go through this struggle, Maren and a team of amazing volunteer creatives created an award-winning video series on cancer à la *Drunk History* called *Confessions of a Caregiver*, which you can find on YouTube. She hopes that this series raises money to end cancer for good.

To learn more go to marenhigbee.com.